DELIRIUM OF INTERPRETATIONS

OTHER BOOKS BY THIS AUTHOR

[with Anthony Howell] *Elements of Performance Art*
   (1996)
London (Sun & Moon Press, 1984)
You — the City (Roof Books, 1990)
oops the join (rempress, 1997)
Cells of Release (Roof Books, 1997)
Hi Cowboy (Mainstream, 1997)

Delirium of Interpretations

Fiona Templeton

GREEN INTEGER
KØBENHAVN & LOS ANGELES
2003

GREEN INTEGER
Edited by Per Bregne
København/Los Angeles

Distributed in the United States by Consortium Book
Sales and Distribution, 1045 Westgate Drive, Suite 90
Saint Paul, Minnesota 55114-1065

First edition 2003
©2003 by Fiona Templeton

This book was published in collaboration with
The Contemporary Arts Educational Project, Inc,
a non-profit corporation, through a matching grant from the
National Endowment for the Arts, a federal agency.

NATIONAL
ENDOWMENT
FOR THE
ARTS

Design: Per Bregne
Typography: Guy Bennett
Cover Photograph: Joanna Eldredge Morrissey
Sculpture Photographs: Anne Schaefer

LIBRARY OF CONGRESS CATALOGING IN PUBLICATION DATA
Templeton, Fiona [1951]
Delirium of Interpretations
ISBN: 1-892295-55-5
p. cm — Green Integer 114
I. Title II. Series

Acknowledgments

This work was originally commissioned in 1990–91 by Claus Donau of Theatre Cocteau-Basel, Basel, Switzerland. It was directed by Michael Ratomski and Claus Donau, with Graziella Rossi, Bettina Grossenbacher, Kamil Krejci, Robert Spitz, Kaja Vrba and Katarina Wilden. Meret Matter, Ulrich Cyran, Bettina Grossenbacher, Andreas Matti and Michael Röhenbach worked as cast in early development, with dramaturgy by Dorothea Koelbing, and direction and concept by Claus Donau.

Revision was made thanks to a Poetry Fellowship from the National Endowment for the Arts, a grant from Art Matters, and residencies at Yaddo, the Lake Placid Institute and MacDowell Colony, and revision development thanks to Michael Ratomski, New Dramatists, Liz Diamond, Lisa Peterson and Lenora Champagne.

Thanks for making situations for writing possible to René Peier, Susanne Mäusli, the Kartause Ittingen artists' retreat, Christoph Renfer, Sybille Herzog and M et Mme Marcel Robert of La Brévine. Thanks also to the latter and to Astrid Schmid, Graziella Rossi and Hannah Hurtzig for helping me get out of them.

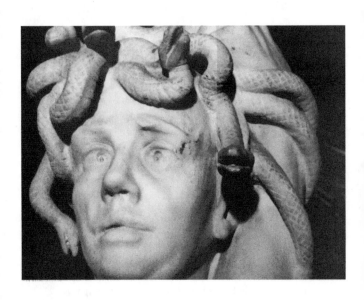

Contents

DELIRIUM OF INTERPRETATIONS

(of the predicament and the phenomenon of Camille Claudel)

CHARACTERS:

C(amille)/subjectivity, (artist)

R(odin, male artist)/(also father, physically)

P(aul), (brother, writer, critic)

M(ere)/Louise/Rose (R's wife)

J(essie/friend/artist/model/"objective" female eye — also sister)

A(rt critic/collector/society/"objective" male eye)

SYNOPSIS:

Narrative: *The play deals with the biography, or rather the conflicting biographies, of the sculptor Camille Claudel (1864–1934). What is known of her is, in brief, that she began sculpting at a precocious age, and met many problems endemic to the clash of career and femininity at that date; she was the pupil and subsequently mistress of Auguste Rodin in his later, acclaimed period; on separating from him she withdrew from society and continued to make art; upon the death of her father, who had always been supportive, she was institu-*

tionalized by her family, including the playwright Paul Claudel, her brother, successful, conventional and religious; she died 30 years later in the asylum, much of her work lost or destroyed.

Delirium of Interpretations *was the contemporary diagnosis given to Camille Claudel's mental illness; now it is known as paranoia.*

"Delirium" can be the crisis of an illness, involving hallucination and illusion, but it can also be the peak of excitement or passion, with the idea of perceiving in a different way. "Interpretations" refers to the subject's understanding of the world. As used in the diagnostic term the plural implies deviation from a norm; but interpretation is also an artist's approach to his or her art, to a character or story or feeling or idea or words or a material. There is also the notion of how many different versions of one story or a person's actions or traces there can be, or judgmental opinions about that; or the critical war of paradigms. In this play, I am not interested in who or what was or should be biographically correct or rational; so this work writes the very excess of subjectivities in all their contradiction. We are all inscribed by prior, interdependent and multiple evidence and interpretations of the world, and participate, creatively or not, in the constant formation of its present and future interpretation, including that of its past.

The historical basis of the play, therefore, is not dealt with as a reality to be approximated but as an example of a phenomenon: broadly speaking, the problem of biography. So Camille Claudel's predicament is seen as one of the bind of interpretation: interpretation of the world by herself, of her by her contemporaries, of both by subsequent biographers, of her work by all of those, of her voice by me, of the text by the actors, of the play and of the phenomenon by its audience, of the patient by the doctor, of women by history, of the individual by the consensus.

TEXT AND STAGING

Notes for reading the play: *The staging of the play and its presentation in the script are part of its theme. Here, therefore, are the major points needed to read the play; they are covered in more depth under details, at the end of the play:*

Only C has an invented or subjective voice—the play is specifically about subjectivity, not biographical objectivity.

Mostly the characters speak in voices borrowed from history. Since reality is multiple, some of these are contradictory in their apparent facts.

Most characters have more than one style or voice, depending on the source; even the same source person may speak differently in a personal letter and in a public speech. Each actor also has an "actor's voice," not necessarily his or her own; the end notes contain some suggestions for improvising these, as some directors/actors may prefer.

Characters often speak simultaneously; this is not a choric simultaneity, but often each speaker means his or her own different reality by the same words, and should be directed separately or ironically (particularly P, whose symbiotic echoing of C only works if it is unconscious).

It should be remembered in reading that characters not speaking may be visible on stage, involved in their own realities; for this reason I have given more suggested directions for P, whose through narrative is less obvious than C's.

Margin notes on sources are given, therefore, as are pictures of sculptures by the main characters, as dramaturgical background, to clarify continuities in the parallel realities. Notes refer to the original speaker or writer; bibliographical references (in brackets) are explained in the end notes, under Details. Sources apply to all text from that point to the next source given, unless otherwise specified.

PROLOGUE

Audience enters — Installation — Talk of actors

The play takes place in a space that refers to several different settings, sometimes simultaneously. These are defined by various configurations of, for example, cinderblocks (or breezeblocks), which also serve as the materials of sculpture, and can thus be moved by the actors.

The audience enters into the performance space as to an exhibition, moving freely about the space with a catalogue as guide to various spots, which are probably not actual works of art — they could as easily be incidental to the space, for example, a pillar, whatever. The actors are dispersed throughout the space, in costume but not in character.

While the audience's initial reaction to the costumes will probably be to establish a distance, the actors should invite closeness and conversation by their normal speaking voices and an obvious non-acting manner. The conversation is specifically in reference to the objects of attention, beginning quite literally but gradually describing them as if they were other predetermined art objects, and also generalizing from those objects to themes connected to the play. This should be rehearsed so that comments appearing later in the text can be incorpo-

rated naturalistically into conversation perhaps apparently initiated by audience members.

Talk about fiction

The level of textual artifice should then gradually move to obvious reference to another reality. For example, J may be looking at a sink and saying "I like this child, this little marble child."

The conversational pitch of speaking allows simultaneity, which means that not everyone in the audience will hear exactly the same comments. However, the scene should last long enough for everyone in the audience to gather the same impression and to hear comments from most of the actors.

In the course of the Prologue, the actors move at the same exhibition-viewing speed as the audience, balancing it to make sure of circulation.

Talk of (family) characters

Within the simultaneity, there is then a transition to characters, where the actors address each other in their roles, though the subject of improvisation remains con-

temporary to the audience, not to the psychological characters, as these are not the primary roles of some of the actors.

This reaches a high pitch of simultaneous argument. This can be quite stylized, in the sense of being stubbornly locked in individual opinion or wish. Some should be contrasting personal phrases from the text, such as A's emphatic "It—is—so," versus J's feeling "It frightens me," or C's slow "I can't... finish... this sentence."

Towards the end of the Prologue, the actors have approached, though not completely, the more specific positions they should take for the Parodos. This is their entry into their characters.

(end of the Prologue)

Camille Claudel, 1884

PARODOS

Notes to the director

The Parodos in Greek theatre is the entry of the chorus, giving background to the action. Here it uses the language of influences on the development of the characters, as background to the action of the main scenes. It covers various stages of C's life up to her encounter with R; thus while the text mainly refers to the myths that formed much of C's education from her father, and that reappear in her sculpture, the action can move from her childhood imagination through her early workplace.

It is very important that simultaneous speakers speak differently rather than in unison. For those actors covering more than one character or aspect of the same character, some distinction of attitude will be useful; lines that will repeat can be identified with specific attitudes and cadences.

It is also important to maintain the different points of view or psychological through lines of those characters not obviously involved in the main textual through line, whether by their reactions or by their separate and co-incidental realities. This is particularly true here of the mother, later of P.

So the Parodos establishes C as the focus, and at the same time the question of whose point of view things are being seen from, either which character's, which source's, which point in time, or the author's, the director's, the actors', or their own.

*At the beginning of the scene C is a child asserting her
imagination; as her playing develops to sculpting, she
may get up from the conversation to consider and change
the physical attitudes of her companions, to place them
in a pose. She should not mime sculpting, rather it
should be clear that she is manipulating her surround-
ings to conform to her reality.*

*P is younger, skulking, part fearful, part trying to as-
sert. J is less competitive, a mixture of "good" and
uninvolved. A is apart from the scene, observing un-
seen, the voice of authority; he regards the women as
aesthetic objects. M is a controlling presence, silent,
suspiciously aware of A; an antagonism with C should
develop in the Parodos.*

C   (*playing with stones:*) The giantess has a man's
    name. In one of her hands is her sheer face, the
    mouth of hole a rocked door in her walls higher
    than a woman's head of loneliness,

C/A (*They look at what she has made, she partly also
     enacting the story.*) standing on the fallen body
     of the giant, who with his left arm is still mak-
     ing a supreme effort to protect his head, which

—(La Geyn [fem.
homonym of
'giant']: desolate,
rock formations
by Claudel home;
cf where PC
banishes
heroines)

-2RMP

23

has been severed by the young hero. The little
David's back has the ridges and ravines of a frag-
ment of an alp.

On early lost
sculpture (*David &
Goliath*)

C   *She* is

C/P/A (*A reads, C enacts as she remembers the words
imperfectly, P recites well but is bossed by C in
playing.*)

-Ovid,
Metamorphoses
[Perseus and the
Gorgon], tr.
author (as all
lines this scene
unless J's or
noted)

a place, chill below Atlas lying,
of solid to be guardianed with armament of mass,
whose in going-in twin inhabited sisters
    (*C makes J be the other sister.*)
daughters of Phorcys, single shared of eye the use.
That Perseus with skills furtively while passed, slyly
with put-in stole with hand.
    (*P identifies with Perseus and C mostly with
the Gorgon, though also occasionally with the
momentarily most exciting character.*)

-author (as all J's
own lines this
scene unless
noted)

J   (*at this point, like a lesson learned:*) Female inaccessibility challenges male transgression.

C   With his other hellish hand, he is

C/P   (*C imperious, P sullen:*) sent to the place known   **-1RMP**
        as the Red Bush to fetch the earth for his sister.

C   the lump his age caresses, as once, that took
        stone's moment, stole, stormed and stormed a
        grain from her lost lip.   **-author**

A   Yes, I mean, art is masculine.   **-A actor**

C/P/A And through said away long
        and path away, and of woodland bristling boul-
            ders of broken,
        of Gorgons gained to home. And throughout
            through fields
        and through ways had seen of men simulacra
            and of beasts (*the audience, M, etc., are im-*
            plicated into a freezing game),
        into stone out of self of sight changed of Medusa.
        He but of horror in shield which on left wore
        in bronze rebounding shape observed of Medusa,
        and while heavy sleep and snakes and herself
            was holding,
        sliced head from neck.

J   and gave it to Minerva (*plays Minerva*), who
           fixed it in the middle of her breastplate.
        What was that snaky-headed Gorgon-shield   **-Milton**

That wise Minerva wore, unconquered virgin,
Wherewith she freezed her foes to congealed
stone,
But rigid looks of chaste austerity!

(M concurs. From here she is less in control of C, as the children grow a little older.)

<table>
<tr><td>-Ovid (as all lines
from here on
unless J's or
noted)</td><td>C/P/A</td><td>He added and far, with not false dangers, journey,</td></tr>
<tr><td></td><td>J</td><td>*(Sarcastic, as are many of her comments in this scene, even slightly resentful:)* Medusa's rest becomes Perseus' glory.</td></tr>
<tr><td></td><td>C/P/A</td><td>*(continuing:)* what seas, what lands under self
had seen from high,
and what with whipped had fondled stars with
wings…
Before expectation fell silent but. Began one
asking why alone she of sisters,
wore meshing incoiled in tresses vipers.
(C enjoys being frightening.)
Perseus replied:…</td></tr>
<tr><td></td><td>C/J</td><td>Most dazzling of figure
and of many was hope jealous of suitors
she, and not in all lovelier any than hair
part was *(J smooths her hair.)*</td></tr>
</table>

A   I've met someone who claimed to have seen   **-1RMP**
        her in those days.

C/P/A Her the sea's ruler in temple raped of Minerva,
        it's said; (*she felt a bird*);
        (*A looks at the girls, then to where R will be.*)

J/P/A averted is and chaste with shield,
        face Minerva covered.

C/P/A And lest this unpunished be,
        Gorgon's hair to vile changed to sea-monsters.

(*C shakes her hair and goes off on her own, becoming absorbed in looking around with great curiosity. P swashbuckles around; he performs slightly for A.*)

J   The sight, not the gaze of Medusa, was her offence. Her hair was her deed. Neptune's violation became Medusa's sin. Her beauty caused her rape and her transformation. The woman desired creates the rock. Her flight was her deed. Her sisters protected, not her, but others from her passive fatality. The sight, not the gaze of Medusa, was her offence. Her ugliness caused death by transformation to stone. Her sisters protected themselves by halving their gaze, and their gaze was stolen. The sight, not the gaze of

27

*Persée et la Gorgone
(detail)*

the Gorgon, was her offence. The woman suffers from the rock she creates. Gaze and sight meet in the mirror. Her ugliness caused her death. The Gorgon's offence became Perseus' power.

28

C/A   (*C begins to sculpt, becomes absorbed.*)
        He himself hands in drawn conquering washes
            in wave,
        and eely head hard not may hurt sand,
        he softens ground with leaves and born below
            water branches,
        he beds, and on lays daughter of Phorcys head
            of Medusa. (*C lays down her head.*)
        Stalks recent and thirsty too now living pore
        power suck of monster and at touch harden his,
        and take unfamiliar in roots and fronds rigor.
        Now also in coral same nature remains,
        and what living in water was, makes above wa-
            ter rock.
        (*C raises her head. The head here will be echoed
           at the beginning of Scene 3.*)

J   Stone flows from Medusa's wound.

(*C and J seem to have their own space now, or may
echo the Causeuses sculpture, while P is now the one
moving around.*)

C/A   He (P) came to a halt in realm Atlantis.
        This of men together in vast body surpassing
        Atlas was. Farthest earth
        kingdom was.

-Photo of Camille
& Louise C &
friend
-Camille C
sculpture *[Les
Causeuses]* (see
p. 98)

29

(Atlas/A here refers to the father, but R also becomes visible at a distance, in his own space, though at this point it should be ambiguous as to who he is, perhaps even a father-reference, echoing M's positions. During the Atlas story, C starts to build something large from the blocks of stone. Future playwright P as Perseus is aware of the drama of the words.)

P   "If glory impresses you of birth great,"

C/A   Perseus said to Atlas,

P   "birth mine Jupiter author;
        or, if you are wondered at feats, are wonderful
           mine.
        Hospitality I ask."

C/A   Reminded Atlas of ancient oracle was…

J   *(She is not so deft with language, self-conscious:)*
        "Time, Atlas, come, your when robbed will be
           of gold
        tree, and of this spoil renown to Jupiter born
           will have."

C/A   To Perseus as to all, he said,

A   "Go away, lest far glory of deeds
      which you lie, far your Jupiter be away."

C/A In virilities weaker Perseus,

P   "Then so small grace to you is mine, take gift!"

C/A said and in left hand apart of Medusa
      self back turning hideous held out head.
      (*P holds his clenched fist towards R, as if coinci-
      dentally, neither aware of the other. C turns her
      head towards P.*)
      As much was, mountain was made, Atlas: for
          beard and hair
      into woods went away, ridges were and shoul-
          ders and arms,
      what head before was, peak was on mountain
          top,
      bones stone became; parts in all
      grew to unmeasure, and whole
      with all stars sky rested on him.

(*Next stage of growing-up. C becomes increasingly serious, working small-scale, on a sculpture with J as
model, throughout the tale of Andromeda. Without C,
P as Perseus puts more attitude into the translation.*)

-Camille C
sculpture [bust
of Louise C - see
photo]

31

P/A The devil star that wakes men to work was high in the heaven of his glittering ascent. Perseus strapped his wings back on, and his weapon, kicked his heels and split the bright air. Around and below he left uncountable peoples till he caught sight of the Ethiopians. There Jupiter Amman had unjustly sentenced harmless Andromeda to pay for the tongue of her mother the queen.

J Female pride deserves the rock?

P/A The minute Perseus saw her (*P acts as if J is the princess*), chained by the arms to the hard rock, he thought she was a marble statue, except that the warm wind moved her hair... He fell so hot and dumb he almost forgot to flap his wings.

P "Tell me your name, and the name of your country, and why you are in chains."

J The female rock is desired.

P/A At first she was silent. She was being a girl, so she did not dare to speak to a man. She would have hidden her face with her modest hands if they hadn't been tied up. She did the only thing she could and filled her eyes with brimming

32

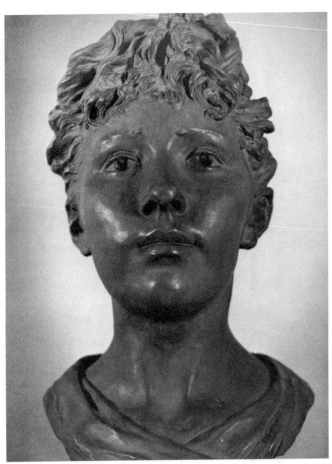

Buste de Louise Claudel, 1885

tears. (J *does not move but her expression is disdainful, unlike what is being verbally imposed on her*.) Perseus insisted, so in case he should think her silence guilty, she told him of her mother's sin of pride in her body. Her father was there, miserable, and her mother too, deservedly so. The stranger said:

P   "If I asked for her, I, Perseus who am born of Jove and the prisoner he filled with his golden rain, I that same Perseus who conquered the wormycurled Gorgon, the man who with beating wings dared ride the wind, of course you'd prefer me as a son-in-law. To the gift of myself I add the gift of saving her." They accepted the deal and threw in a kingdom and a fortune.

J   Male pride deserves the woman.

P/A   Look, here comes the monster like a sharp-snouted ship cleaving the sea, attacking Perseus' shadow! *(Skipping the action scene.)* Three, four times and again he sticks his sword in its guts. The parents celebrate and call Perseus son. The girl falls in, freed from her chains, his prize…

J/A   (*J sarcastically:*) "Now, bravest Perseus, tell us
       with how much valor and with what skill you
       plucked off that serpent-locked head."

J   (*whispering like a crowd:*) "Show us the head,   -Hawthorne, *The*
       show us the head..." shouted the people.   *Gorgon's Head*

A   (*continuing:*) Perseus replied,...

P   "a place, chill below Atlas lying,"

J   So Medusa hid below the slopes of Atlas *before
       Perseus* made Medusa create the slopes of At-
       las? Get over yourself, hero. (*C and J laugh.*)

P   (*rejected so disdaining:*) Then having nothing   -Paul C, *My*
       better to do, I went back to mass. (*Disengages*   *Conversion*
       himself with effort from the action, kneels and
       closes his eyes, facing away; he stays like this into
       the next scene, desperate for his own world.)

C/A   (*Grown up; now her fantasy, the "adult" trans-*
       lation, though A makes subtext more explicit
       than she:) Pomona loves country things, and   -Ovid
       trunks loaded with fertile fruit. (*C is working*   (Vertumnus &
       on something with P as model.) Not with a mis-   Pomona)

Jeune Romain, 1884 (Paul Claudel à 16 ans)

sile is she laden but she holds the hooked sickle in her hand. This she uses to curb over-luxuriousness or to control limbs that are spreading everywhere. She inserts a twig into an incision in the bark, and lends its juices to a nursling of a different nature. She cannot bear that they might feel thirsty, and waters the curling fibers of the roots that drink her lapping streams. This is her love, this her passion, and no desire for mating. But for fear of countryboy violence she hides inside her fruitgrove and prohibits access and takes refuge from men.

(Builds a kind of wall, to be echoed at the end of Scene 4.)

-Camille C sculpture [bust of Paul C at 16 - see photo]

P   *(in his own religious thing:)* Pax! pax! pax!

-Paul C, Angelus in *L'Annonce Faite à Marie*

J   Female inaccessibility challenges male trangression.

C/A   *(while R appears gradually, but remaining apart, also working, perhaps casually moving things:)*
What didn't the young dancers do, or the horny ones, or the terror of sinners by hook or by cock, to overpower her? Even Vertumnus, the greatest lover, was no luckier. At last through his many disguises he discovered how to get in. Holding out his curved hook, he was a leaf-

-Ovid

37

gatherer or vine-cutter; he wore ladders: you'd suppose he went to pick fruit. He sprinkled grey hair at his temples, and leaning on his rod he entered the tended garden and admired her fruit. There was an elm tree resplendent with glowing grapes. (A *may dominate as Vertumnus' voice*.) "But if," he said, "the trunk stood celibate without the young vine, it would have nothing to show but its leaves. And this vine that has become one with it is resting on the elm; if it was not married to it, it would trail awry on the earth. But you are unmoved by the tree's example, and you run from sex and you're not looking for attachment. But if you're wise, choose Vertumnus for a bed partner. Count this: his gift of natural grace, and how he will fit himself into all shapes, and whatever you command, (and you have license to command anything), he will become. (*P looks around, and away again.*) What you like, he prefers, and he'll hold your gifts with joy in his hand. Pity his burning and believe that he is here begging with my lips for what he wants. Be with your lover." In the shape of age he pleads in vain. He changes back to a young man and shows himself to her. (*Still apart, R steps back from his work at the same time as C steps back from hers.*)

A   It's pure Rodin! (*Attributing her work (in the shape of P) to Rodin.*)   -1RMP (said of C's work before she knew of R)

J/A   He is ready to force,

        (*R moves closer into sight. C looks, not at him, but at what he has been working on.*)

C/A   but force is not needed. The girl is ravished at the sight of him and feels an answering wound.

J   (*While C moves to Scene One:*)
        Earth outgrows the mythic fancies
        Sung beside her in her youth.   -Elizabeth Barrett Browning (contemporary of Camille C)

        (*end of the Parodos*)

39

SCENE ONE

QUOTED FROM
(SOURCE IN
BRACKETS)

R's factory-like studio, full of activity and material. The
audience is treated by R as models, in a proprietory,
though not unappreciative way; or as students by A,
who here speaks as Gsell, R's biographer. J is also pos-
ing or drawing. C is there as a student. P remains as at
the end of the Parodos until pulled in by C. Although P
& R ignore each other as characters, there is a certain
competitiveness.

M is now the one who is outside of the main reality; she
sits solidly, busy with some handwork, as if not aware
of the other reality though her actions sometimes coin-
cide with what happens there.

A	In his workplace several nude models walk about or rest.	-Gsell, Rodin's biographer (G26)
R	The sculptor compels the spectator to follow the development of the act in the individual.	-Rodin (G71)
A	He pays them to furnish him constantly with the sight of the nude moving with all the freedom of life,	-Gsell (G26)
R	not only fleeting gestures, but a long action. (*As he speaks to everyone, he places the other actors*	-Rodin (G82)

43

in relative standing positions, though not poses, so allowing them to move, in which they are independent, but constituting a group sculpture; he occasionally stops them by grasping their legs or arms, rather roughly. C considers his words, then quietly places J, M and A in the relative positions for L'Âge Mûr, but the action flows soon out of this—it's just a foreshadowing. Then she

L'Âge Mûr, 1895

brings P to stand in front of her. His gaze is fervent but jealous, hers professional.) He needs   -Rodin (G85)
only to place his characters in such a manner
that the spectator shall first see those who begin this action, then those who continue it, then
those who complete it. You will no longer say
that painting and sculpture are unable to compete with theatre. *(Until "Yeah," he walks around
it all, considering, sometimes part of it, commenting to himself.)*

   …Such a work is worth a whole biography.   -Rodin (G125)
   …And the people of the day, almost elbowing   -Rodin (G89)
them.

(C walks behind P, caressing his face and head, sometimes lovingly, sometimes professionally, as if sculpting.)

P   You place! you clayed and cloying earth! here,   -Paul C, *Tête*
my feet in the earth, the wind sticks a mask of   *d'Or,* 17
rain on me. What did I repeat in my silence? I   -Paul C, *T d'O* 21
will be able. *(C makes him kneel. He closes his*
eyes.) I am like a man below the earth. But not   -Paul C, *T d'O* 28
a twig but delirium enters like a creator, pro-   -Paul C, *T d'O* 29
ducing flower and seed. I vibrate like a pole, *(R*   -Paul C, *T d'O* 34
walks by, touching the head, professionally.) in
the fury of the male, *(P grasps R's hands, eyes*

45

-Paul C, *T d'O* 35		*still closed.*) and there is no woman in me. See, I will not give you back your hands. (*R is looking at C, then walks away.*)
-Rodin (G89)	R	But my proposal was rejected. They insisted upon a pedestal.
-Paul C, *T d'O* 38	P/C	You knelt in front of me.
-attrib. director Lugne-Poe *Cahiers PC*, 80	J	His words are too beautiful to be put on the lips of an actor.
-R actor	R	Yeah, I'm sorry about the pauses
-A actor	A	where the artist in fact builds a mediating character, between his role and his self, for which he can't be fully open to criticism.
-R actor	R	In theatre it would be very boring to have such long pauses. But now we're here to work. (*He faces A. He should probably have something to touch, full-handedly.*)
-author	C/A	Imagine a passive body that pays attention to an active body. Imagine an active body that pays attention to a passive body.

R   Instead of imagining the different parts of a body as surfaces more or less flat, I represented them as projections, to express in each swelling the efflorescence of a muscle or bone beneath the skin, as the point, more or less large, which it directs towards you. (*An as yet disinterested unconscious sexual reference.*)

-Rodin (G59)

A   On this face there were absolutely no symmetrical planes, nothing was repeated, no place remained empty, dumb, or indifferent. On this head there was no line, no intersection, no contour that he had not seen and willed. What was written on the face could be read on the smallest part of the body; each place was a mouth saying it in its way.

-Rilke (K5) on Rodin's [*Homme au Nez Cassé*]

-Rilke on Rodin's [*L'Âge d'Airain*]

P   I didn't dare open my mouth.

-Paul C, *My Conversion*

(*During the next part, that is, R's text with C's text down to the mention of the Höllentor, the two texts are not dramatically interlinked but parallel, in a more musical or intertextual way. They can occasionally be almost simultaneous.*)

R   oh… now I see,

-R actor

47

-author

C   Someone's in the room. Be pure! Be partial.

-these 2
continue to
alternate

R   on this man's chest, another face…

C   Fragmentary not in the sense of more where this comes from, but incompleted by attention.

R   like an owl, a really sad, depressive old owl…

C   And incompleted not in the sense of a whole, but what does the model attend to?

R   no, I mean, maybe the face is the shape of the lungs or something…

C   She is reading a book she partially understands.

R   but that's interpretation, that's not important…

C   Her familiarity with its language meets equivalence,

R   But, it is really strong…

C   but each of its abstract terms seems to mean abstract.

R   And now I see underneath, too…

OOOOHHHH, THAT'S NOT TO BE BE-
LIEVED...

C A landscape evolves where she cannot distin-
guish the structure of space, a specific space,
from the structure of time, a specific time.

R underneath, underneath, on the belly, there's
like another screaming face.

C Later she is not sure if this is the meaning of
the book, or of the white stone, or of the impor-
tance of the white stone, or of the pain when
she moves again, or of the hysteria of uncom-
plicated concentration, or of the relief of un-
regulated brain activity,

R Well, they are definitely faces, like eaten away
with cancer or something;

C or of the soldiers who may be looking from the
castle windows, or of her small body seen by
the soldiers, or of her silver hands.

R or sickness of the lungs, internal sickness.

C Move my hands at the speed your blood can.

49

R   This man has like three faces;

C   Turn this thigh.

R   himself,…

C   I turn her thigh. I bend his neck into the mud.

R   But I'm moving into the realm of interpretation…

C   Her breath tightens which shoulder. His eyes close my fingers from what I see,

R   NOW I SEE ANOTHER FACE on the,

C   or of the marks on her body of the reading of the book

R   on the hip, on the hipjoint, another little face…

C   She knows that it is not written in my language.

R   So yes… it doesn't matter, if it's intended or not…

C   My rubbing reads a bone into her back.

R I SEE ANOTHER FACE, oh, there's no
   question…

C My palm flattens on what I can't make.

R That's great… That's great… it's great.

C She looks back.

R (*Moves away.*) And so I have to make my door
   to Hell,

   -Gates of Hell,
   [Höllentor] Rodin
   sculpture

A at which he worked, all alone, for twenty years.

   -Rilke (K16)

C Is this a true story? I don't know yet.

   -author (Rodin
   had many
   helpers
   including Camille
   C)

(*R catches sight of C again. He looks at her work (P),
then at her.*)

P What did I repeat in my silence?

   -Paul C, *T d'O*, 21

R I have what I make.

   -author

C I make what I am. I have made a chink to the
   back of the world.

-Paul C, *T d'O,* 12   P   Look at me, I need and I don't know what, and I could shout it forever.

-author   C   My brother and I invented a language.

-Paul C, *T d'O*   P   No, may this plea not be denied me.

-author   C   Yes, you do, aren't you? Yes, you are, don't you?

-Paul C, *T d'O* 54
-P actor   P   We are unable to be able. I have to get totally on top of it. What does on top of it mean?… Okay I do need someone to tell me what to do. And I've seldom met people who really said to me: Do that. And I really enjoyed it; and it was difficult. Mostly it was easy. What does mostly

-Paul C, *T d'O,* 40   mean? No, it was always difficult. To do, do, do! Who will give me the strength to do?

-author (Camille C made hands for Rodin, who was less skilful at them)   R   Make me hands…

(C takes P's hand, and works it.)

   R   and feet.

(C looks down but will not kneel.)

-Paul C, *Vers d'Exil*   P   One must submit to the master. Someone in me more myself than myself.

Étude de main, 1885

R The modern spirit upsets and breaks all forms in which it takes body.   -Rodin (G218)

C My feet are huge, my hands are huge, and I have swallowed the world.   -author

R (*to J:*) With a certain laugh young girls can strangely disarm success, and what's more they're right.   -Rodin (1RMP57)

P A man received, in spite of himself, the call of God, a call that cannot be repudiated.   -Paul C on himself, *Partage de Midi,* Preface, 10

(*R has been walking around the space, stopping others in painful positions. Then he rearranges C and P with P kneeling facing C, eyes still closed.*)

-Rodin (q.John Berger—ref as Be)	R	The first thing God thought of when he made the world, was modeling with the earth.

-Paul C on himself as above	P	After a long resistance, dragging by the leash his trembling will, he presented himself at the altar, and it was from God himself that he had his reply. (*He freezes, eyes closed, in wait.*)

-Rodin (Be)	R	No good sculptor can model a human form without coming to an understanding of the mystery of life. This and any individual, with its fleeting variations, reminds him of the basic type it contains; from the creation he is constantly led to the creator. (*This refers first to C sculpting, then to himself*).

(*R goes behind C and takes her arms behind her, and holds her legs together with the other arm, as if making a pose, or as if to stop her making P.*)

-[*The Hand of God*] a cast by Rodin of his own hand	R	(*He also pulls P's arms around his back, so that C & P form* [*L'Eternelle Idole*]*.*) The Hand of God.

R   (*Looks at what he has made, then, honestly:*)
We're not made of wood. (*Then repeats this to
A as if it is a title.*) We're not made of wood.

-[We're not made of wood] R's first name for his [*L'Eternelle Idole*]

A   With the devotion
of the priest for his idol.

-Baudelaire's "L'Hostie," the first public name for [*L'Eternelle Idole*]

R   The Host.

A   And I cherish, oh cruel and implacable beast!
This very coldness that makes you more beautiful.

-B's "L'Hostie"

R   The Eternal Idol. (*Looks at them again.*)

C/A   Sometimes he murmured the names of his statues, but one felt that the names meant little to him. He ran his hand over their surfaces, caressed them, all the while breathing heavily.

-Isadora Duncan on Rodin (*My Life*)

R   It is truly flesh! You almost expect the body to be warm when you touch it.

-Rodin (Be)

P   (*He remains in place while R's attention has
turned to C's body. P says this as if subconsciously, then as the actor, not the character,
while the character still waits for his reply:*) Do

-P actor

not touch! I'd like more than anything to touch these things.

-Isadora Duncan
as above

c/(j) Then I began to explain to him, but I soon realized that he wasn't listening. He was staring at me from under half closed lids, his eyes were sparkling, and then he came towards me, with the same expression on his face as he had for his statues. He ran his hands over my hips, my naked legs and feet. He began to knead my whole body in such a way as if it consisted of clay, while he gave off a heat that seared me and melted me inside.

-Paul C,
L'Annonce Faite
à Marie, 12

c/p I'm not afraid of you, mason! You don't get to the end of me just the way you'd like!

-Paul C on
himself (Partage
de Midi, Preface)

p (*At last, the awaited reply.*) Clear. A pure and simple refusal, peremptory, accompanied by no explanation.

-Ovid
Metamorphoses
(Pygmalion) (Be)

R/A Pygmalion makes for the image of his girl, and
      bending over
the bed surrenders kisses to her. She seems
      warm; he moves
his mouth on hers again and feels her breasts
      with his hands:

the ivory melts to the touch, and its hardness
    hollows and yields
where he places his fingers, as wax from
    Hymetus softens in the sun
and kneaded with the thumbs can be bent and
    shaped and made usable with use.

C/P   Doormaker, let me open this one for you.

-Paul C, *L'A F à M*, 17

P   And the Word was made flesh.

-Paul C, *P de M*

A/R   Flesh of the woman, ideal clay, o wonder,
       Oh sublime penetration of the spirit
       In the slime kneaded by the ineffable Being.

-Victor Hugo quoted in G118

(R gradually takes P's place.)

P   He is eliminated.

-Paul C on himself, *P de M*

A/R   Matter where the soul shines through its shroud
       Mud where one sees the fingers of the divine
       sculptor.

-Victor Hugo as above, cont'd.

P   *(Disgustedly:)* Deliver the goods.

-PC compares R's *Eternelle Idole* to C's *Sakountala/ V&P* (JC393)

*(C finishes rearranging herself and R into [Sakountala]/
[Vertumnus and Pomona].)*

-Kalidasa (*Sakountala*), k15	C/A	An unknown power oppressed my whole be-ing.
-Paul C as above	P	(*More appreciatively:*) The second before con-tact.
-Kalidasa (K18)	C/A	Rise, Lord!

(*R gets up, still holding C by some part of the body as if it is separate from her. P's interpretation of the lines from his plays here can either hold him into identifica-tion with R or C, or begin his more separate identity by continuing his elimination and search for one who will command him.*)

-Paul C, *L'A F à M*, 76	P/R	I hold you for good, your hand and the arm with it, and everything that comes with the arm.

(*From here to before their unison line, R & C are mu-tually, though differently as in the text, sculpting each other.*)

-Mathias Morhardt, contemp critic of R&C (JC448) -Be 116 -2RMP -K	A	He never worked in marble, and left it to his assistants to hew such a self-willed material. She undertakes a portrait, immediately and without prior sketch, directly out of a block of stone. His forms are so reduced that they are no longer independent, they are oppressed. He makes her

emerge from the stone, she liberates her. For her this woman is the hunter, for him, the captive. She catches and gathers light, whereas he presents a compact mass that repels it; she is filigreed, she has cuts.   -2RMP

C   And let this air represent air, through which you can arrive more quickly. I discovered it over me, that the relation between you and here was an imparting, a reversal and re-reversal from material to impulse to material via the impulse and via the body, to the body, to the impulse, and this didn't represent air by being surrounded or covered or shifted, perfectly short of perfection because without repetition, by repetition, and what had been surface and what had been immobile became a muscle of motive, parts of the body scratched out, parts of speech wetted on, down in the science of severance embedding completion as if emerging?   -author

R   In love the only thing that counts is the sex act. What joy that in my work I can both love and speak of my love!   -Rodin (Be)

R/C   (*to each other, C catching R's last lines, R catching her reaction:*) What do you ask? I ask everything. I ask everything of you, for you to give it   -Paul C, *T d'O*, 125

to me, so that this power of everything be mine,
to do everything and to have everything.

end of scene 1

(*the action, however, continues directly*)

SCENE TWO

Notes to the Director

Just as the introduction of R's wife to C's family is a complex mix of roles, so also the similarity in the conflicting accounts from the biographies as to whether C haunted R's footsteps or viceversa, or M did, can be staged to emphasise their repetitiveness and the conflict of subjectivities.

Otherwise the other actors remain peripheral to R and C's drama.

*Same time and place. R begins in reply to C's last line
of the previous scene.*

*R is trying to lead C both to work (for him) and to se-
duce her out of working (for herself) and into retreat.
The retreat area of the stage could be kind of separate,
as it would allow R & C to be out of reach there while
he can come down and be public.*

R   Here is a ladder.

-author

*(C climbs a few steps to work, R walks around laying
his hands on a few other "statues." He goes to her, covers up her body somehow.)*

R/A   (A reading:) You should crown my frieze of the
damned, but you I cannot show naked. And yet
above this Door, you could not be otherwise.

-Rodin in a letter
(2RMP40)

R   I don't see angels as bodies, only heads. Here is
a head.

-Rodin (G)
-author

A/P   The image of my sister in the body of a young
man.

-(conflicting
critical
interpretations
of CC's sculpture
[*Gorgon*])

A   Her face is the brother.

63

Persée et la Gorgone (detail)

-Paul C, *Partage de Midi* 89-90

P/C   Am I a man?

P/R   Don't be a madwoman.

P/C   And yet I have arms and legs like any other and I can answer when you speak to me.

-Paul C, *P de M* 91

P/R   You are as beautiful as Apollo.

P   You are straight as a pillar.

P/A/R   Apollo, God of the door, you have destroyed me.

-Aeschylus: Cassandra in *Agamemnon,* PC in Racine

C   The true giant of the woman's name has a man's name.

-author

A   An example of the head is still exhibited under a usurped name, rising inextricable from the two histories.

-RMP (2RMP109)

R   In each of these two beings one follows the struggle between two natures which progressively invade and supplant each another,

-Rodin (G68)

P   in an interpenetration beyond words, in the voluptuousness of difference,

-PC, *P de M* 146

(From here on, P moves, physically and psychologically, though at first with difficulty, towards his own world, spiritual or imaginary—in fact he conflates the two. Perhaps he is sublimating into his writing.)

P/C   and I am a man in you, and you are a woman with me. It needn't be very loud, but if you were to call me by my name, by your name, there is a woman in me who could not stop herself from answering you.

-PC, *P de M* 87
-PC, *P de M* 54

-PC, *P de M* 86 P/R What can I call you? A mother, because you are good to have. And a sister, and I hold your round arm between my fingers. And a prey, and heavy, and swollen, and forbidden in the hand of her enemy,

-PC, *Mes Idées sur le Théâtre* P (*Detaching a little psychologically:*) On the contrary, I see her face to face with her prey, and holding him by the wrists.

-PC, *T d'O* R One day I took her neck in my two hands.

-Les Frères Goncourt, contemporary diarists (1RMP110-12) A (*while R introduces her to A:*) ...this evening with his pupil, with her childish face, her beautiful eyes, her original talk, her country heaviness of speech,

-Louise Claudel, Camille's mother, in a letter to C (1RMP31) M (*as if a continuation. The complexity of moves here is appropriate:*) the ignoble comedy you played us. (*M is the mother with the family (J and P) being introduced to R:*) I, naive enough to invite the great man, (*M moves to the other side.*) with the woman you called by his name, (*then M momentarily plays R's older mistress being introduced to the family!*) his concubine! And you (C), all sugar, living with him as a kept woman.

C/P   (*Some of P's lines, such as this one, may be said while he is writing them as author.*) I am the promise that cannot be kept. Happy the woman who has found who to give herself to. She won't ask to have herself back. But who really needs her and not another just as much?

-Paul C, *La Ville* (1RMP38)
-PC, *P de M* 60

R   (*Lusts after all the women, including audience.*) Everywhere, the great artist hears spirit answer to his spirit. So, all the masters advance to the barrier which parts us from the Unknowable. (*to, and as if meaning C. Pause. Then he looks at and approaches J.*)

-Rodin (G179)
-Rodin (G183)

A   He comes all the way here to hide from the woman who adores him. (*R gets carried away, then goes over to A.*)

-RMP (1RMP58)

R   The word artist means to me the man who takes pleasure in what he does. This is because the artist, full of feeling, can imagine nothing that is not endowed like himself. (*Slight lewd reference. He faces C.*) Make me heads.

-Rodin (G223)
-Rodin (G166)

-author

A   (*While C touches R's head:*) The architecture of the face is centered on the brow of an Atlas carrying the whole world, the domination of the creator over the tortured temples, the jutting

-(2RMP120 on Camille C's [*Bust of Rodin*])

Buste de Rodin, 1888

arcades of the brows protecting the extinguished myopic eyes and protruding nose of the great sensualist.

R   I can speak of the body, and as my speech copies the body, my only ambition is to be servilely faithful to her.   -Rodin (G130)

P   It is urgent, it is necessary that I be as completely, as intensely as possible, myself.   -Paul C, *Emmaüs*

R   Finally, view in profile the convexity of the back of the statue, in form like a C.   -Rodin (G213)

P   To become a new and formidable being, to pronounce one's "I."   -Paul C, *My Conversion*

R   (*Noticing P:*) How charming! This young torso, without a head, seems to smile at the light and spring, better than eyes and lips could do.   -Rodin (G213)

A   (*Looking at C:*) You would think she slept, did not the anguish in her face betray the conflict in her spirit. The most surprising thing, however, is that it has neither arms nor legs. It would seem that the sculptor in a moment of discontent with himself had broken them off.   -Gsell (G151)

-Rodin (G151)	R	What do you mean? My figure represents Meditation. That's why it has neither arms to act nor legs to walk.
-Gsell (G162)	A	Master, now the symbol is easily understood. Thought expands within the breast of inert matter.
-Rodin (G153)	R	What right have they to forbid me to add meaning to form?
-author	C/A	I will read you your rights.
-an actual contract between Rodin and Camille C (H119)	C/R	From today onwards I will accept no pupils other than her so that no rival talent might accidentally emerge, though I don't imagine one often comes across such naturally gifted artists; for four or five months, from now till May, I will have no other woman, or else the conditions will be broken; I will take no other female models that I have known; after the exhibition, we will leave for Italy, the beginning of an insoluble relationship, after which Mlle will become my wife;
-Ibsen, *When We Dead Awaken* (3rd person) (said to be inspired by R &	R/A	the living wet clay will be what she loves, as it grows out of the raw mass into a vivid creature; she will go on till the end of her days tiring herself to death with lumps of clay and blocks of stone.

(R *whispers in C's ear, perhaps in the position of* L'Abandon *again.*)

Çacountala, 1905 (L'Abandon)

71

La Niobide Blessée, 1906

A And the male mouth murmurs in the ear this secret of love that wipes away all offence. (*C whispers in R's ear, possibly in the position of The Sculptor and the Muse.*) The Muse that stimulates the sculptor and talks in his ear has both an erotic power and an intellectual power. She is not a consoling Muse but a torturing one.

-Baudelaire as above

-[*Sculptor/Muse*] R sculpture - pose like [*L'Abandon*] -(K50) Caso/ Sanders, Rodin catalogue 1977

P I separate myself from you, sister that I have called by an unholy name.

-Paul C, *Emmaüs*

R The great artist finds in the sight of suffering something which fills him with a voluptuous though tragic admiration. When he sees all youth fading, all strength failing, all genius dying, more than ever he rejoices in his knowledge and he is happy. His ecstasy is terrifying.

-Rodin (G49-50)

C/A No doubt an obstacle has prevented the fruit of the good works of my former existences from having effect, since my husband, so full of goodness, became cruel. (*R walks away, leaving her as* La Niobide Blessée.)

-Kalidasa as above (K15)

A The body is similar to the body of a female figure in couples,

-[*La Niobide Blessée*] Camille C sculpture, like the female in [*L'Abandon*] -author

C but the hand that half-shielded the breast grasps

too late at an arrow. But this didn't happen in
any of the stories, so

-Ovid (Niobe)   C/A   mourning dress, and hair let streaming down.
One sank dying, her face on her brother's, while
pulling the arrow that pierced to the

-author   C   (*From being the figure she makes the figure.*) surface of her metal difference from the other fe-
male figures, but in the language the eye sur-
veys till the body identifies, and the time of the
wound is the time of the language, after the
language of the time, and to tell you the time,
left it to tell you how long it takes and how each
blow of your man's arm on your woman's arm
tells you how you carry always your bones inside you, and each raising of your man's shoulder tells the skin of the stone how its woman's
wrist means the arrow, and how her whole arm
drops to abandon the pain of making the drop.
What the moment of this woman's body surrenders is time. If you can't leave your body you
might as well leave it the privilege,

-Ovid (Vertumnus   C/A   (*as C and R move away from each other:*) she
& Pomona)   hides inside her fruitgrove and prohibits access.

C	Everything is mown, hay, corn, oats. You can walk around, it's delightful. If you are good and keep your promise, we will reach heaven. I'll sleep naked to make myself believe you're here, but when I wake up it's no longer the same. I kiss you. Above all stop deceiving me.	-Camille C, letter to Rodin (JC84/1RMP47)
R	(*with a roving eye on the audience:*) I told her I was looking for his face.	-Rodin re Balzac sculpture
C/P	I am the one who should always have been his wife and not her! Go and tell her she mustn't marry him or I'll kill myself!	-Paul C, *L'Annonce Faite à Marie* 60
C/P/M	And must this man who belongs to me be cut in two? And must this child that was mine be cut in two?	-Paul C, *L'A F à M* 211
C	No corpse. No crime. We never fell because there is still landscape, and because a womb has no gravity.	-author
P/C	Oh how one feels like a woman when one is with one's child! Ah, I feel a stiff little body! This milk cooking in my breasts, Jeanne, she's called.	-Paul C, *P de M* -Paul C, *L'A F à M* 168 -Paul C, *L'A F à M* 138

-Paul C, *L'A F à M* 93	R/P	It's not my fault that you're not a man and that I take what's yours. (*P's being on the male and the female sides of this dialogue is the problem he confronts partly by writing it.*)
-Paul C, *L'A F à M* 169	C/P	Do you think I have fifty children to tear out of my body? Do you know what it is to rip yourself in two and put out this screaming little being?
-Paul C, *M I sur T*	P	The consonant, not the vowel, should take the stress. It is much more emphatic to say, instead of …this screeeeeaaaaaming little being, …this ssscrrrrrreaming little being.
-J actor (on CC's [*La Petite Châtelaine*]) -Morhardt (2RMP141) on the same -Paul C, *M I sur T*	J	I like this child. (*Sympathetic but ineffectual*).
	A	I have bought the little mad girl.
	P	The child should never be seen, simply suggested under a voluminous shawl.
-J actor	J	I like this little marble child, the ears, and especially the hair, how it falls down over the back, then on one side and on the other side, in two parts, and I feel in it some longing for being young, for being innocent, unspoiled.

La Petite Châtelaine, 1896

C/P   We're going to blow through the roof! The dog,   -Paul C, *P de M,*
       the cat, and you, and me, and the bastard with   111-112
       us! (*Such lines are, for P, identifying with his
       characters in spite of himself, influenced by the
       reality of his sister.*)

-Rodin letter to Camille C (HC120)	R	I am crying and you doubt me.
-Camille C letter to Rodin (JC123)	C	I'm sure you overdid the food again in your cursed dinners, with the cursed crowd I hate, that takes your health and gives you nothing in return.
-Rodin letter to Camille C (H120)	R	My ferocious friend, my poor head is quite sick, and I cannot get up in the morning.
-Camille C letter to Rodin (JC83)	C	As for my health I am no better because I cannot stay in bed, having all the time reasons to walk.

(Everybody gradually starts prowling around everybody else, contradictorily.)

-Rodin letter to Camille C (H120)	R	Why didn't you wait for me?
-Camille C letter to Rodin (JC83) -Camille C (1RMP331)	C	I was absent because my father came. There is always something missing.
-RDescharnes, contemp (JC186)	A	*(As if writing or thinking this:)* She (C) comes prowling around his villa, and, in the evening, crouching in the bushes, stalks his return.
-Paul C, *P de M*	C/P	Don't be absent in the middle of my life.

78

R	This evening I wandered for hours without finding you,	-Rodin letter to Camille C (HC120)

P	Who has set in motion, said God, this certain lack, this absence in everything? I did, said Wisdom.	-Paul C, *Ode for Dante*

C	(*To R:*) Whatever you do, don't come near my workplace.	-Camille C letter to Rodin (JC126)

A	If he came home late, his wife (*M*), intoxicated with jealousy, burning with ideas of vengeance, was prowling like a madwoman, in the night, around their house, stalking the step on the road of the loved and hated man,	-Judith Cladel essay (she interviewed Rodin) (K53)

R	(*still to C*): our places, in spite of the madness I feel coming on, which will be your work.	-Rodin letter to Camille C (HC120)

R/A	It is marked, in the same place, on the left side of the neck, now with my (*A says "his"*) signature.	-RMP (2RMP105) (put into 1st person)

C/P	(*C bitterly about R, P possessively about himself:*) Anyone who didn't agree that he was the author couldn't come to the meeting. (*P again tries to separate towards his own struggle.*)	-author

-Ibsen, as above	C/A	After that word I left you. I should have killed that child before I left you. I should have crushed it — pounded it to dust. (*Mild prefiguring of the breaking gestures to appear at the end of Scene 4.*) There's no resurrection of a partnership like ours.
-R and Louise C both attributed (1RMP113, 1RMP101)	M/R	I have no more authority over her.
-Ibsen, as above	C/A	You had no more need of my life.
-Rodin (G141)	R	All the activity that is expended in acquiring useful relations is lost to art.
-author	C	I live only with also, but the struggle to be also only is deadly. All of my names are things taken by actions. Abandon. The little keeper of keys.
-A actor	A	Power/powerlessness… I'm beginning to think some things about my characters, well about the critic, insofar as er… this go-between, and then this dilemma, why, tell me, when I see things and have an opinion about them and a feeling and a clear expression, why can I not do them myself? Why don't I myself act, why don't I myself sculpt, why don't I myself compose? (*Propelled into the action more, or maybe C has been sculpting him.*)

R   I regret nothing. Not even the end, which seems funereal. I owe you everything, the share of heaven I've had in my life. Leave your hands on my face. Night later, night after.

-Rodin letter to Camille C (HC121)

C   Apparently I go out at night through the window of my tower.

-Camille C letter to Rodin (JC83)

A   (*Referring to himself:*) She left her workplace only with him. Their flesh was young, beating with life. (*They waltz to Debussy's La Valse, in the form of Camille C's sculpture of the same name. A is Debussy here.*) The group is the turning of two beings, this langour and this drive mingled in a single rhythm, joined in the very eye of the wind. I thought I did well by asking her to clothe her characters, but the drapery surrounds and winds them, flapping like a shroud, words that should never have been said, false notes crashing against those that sang in me. She would never take certain steps, those that demand the whole soul. Was it a dream I loved? And the splendid bath of hair disappears into brightness and trembling, o stones! Her neck and even her chin are still held in the heavy block of marble from which they cannot get free. (*Without overdoing it, maybe R has intervened. Gloomily.*)

-Goncourt (2RMP34)

-Bourdeau, contemp critic (2RMP129)
-RMP on C C sculpture [*La Valse*] (2RMP128-9)
-Dayot, contemp critic (2RMP127)

-Bourdeau as above

-Debussy, who courted Camille C, (1RMP63)
-Mallarme *L'Après-Midi d'un Faune* (also a Debussy work)
-Gsell (G161)

La Valse, 1905

A/R L'Adieu and La Convalescente, worked on as if by a bird, from above, emphasise pathetically the sinking of his companion, the body followed by the head, wrecked without a call for help, becoming engulfed.

-RMP (2RMP40) [sculptures by R, modeled by C C, of heads just emerging from stone]

C (*to R:*) Would you be sweet and buy me a little bathing costume, a dark blue two-piece with white trim, size medium?

-Camille C letter to Rodin (2RMP47)

end of scene 2
(*again the action continues although it shifts*)

Notes to the director

C begins the scene inside her work, as it were. So there is a lot of sculptural/imaginative action.

SCULPTURES:
When positions relating to the sculptures are described, this doesn't mean that the action is purely symbolic. In fact these positions would be better as emerging from, or coincidental moments of, otherwise more naturalistic action.

I borrow Reine-Marie Paris' characterization of Camille Claudel's sculpture after her separation from Rodin, as the "infernal" work (full-sized nightmarish pieces like Clotho, the Gorgon) and the "everyday" (the Causeuses and other tiny works).

In the everyday action, mostly women only. Definitely not R.

In the infernal action, Clotho is M, becoming the older woman in L'Âge Mûr. But C should also be Clotho, in positions that later become the Gorgon. Maybe C should also therefore play both sides of L'Âge Mûr in a second version. In the Gorgon, A plays Perseus. However, earlier, C has played David to Goliath (A or R, or even, by force, P?), and the Gorgon should echo this reversal. The Niobide Blessée *(previous scene) could also have echoed this, while being* Sakountala *alone. R here is only in* L'Âge Mûr. *P himself, later, though in* Sakountala *preceded R (Scene 1). This will all make sense in 4 dimensions, in reference to the sculptures!*

QUOTED FROM
(SOURCE IN
BRACKETS)

The scene break, though again the action and text follow directly, marks the practical separation of C and R. C has moved inside her work, as it were.

A (*beginning questioningly, as if continuing the request of the end of Scene* 2:) with hair twisting extravagantly like snakes over the shoulders, leaning forwards as the hands, wanting forwards as the belly, animated like a garland of seaweed, giving the young girl the look of a drowned man.

-RMP on Camille
C sculpture
[*L'Implorante*]
(2RMP167)

C Slippage, upturn, danger, scoop.

-author

J And especially the hair, it's so nicely braided, and she has such thick hair. I was always jealous of thick hair, because mine was so stringy.

-J actor

P/C May I not be forgiven if I'm not ready to shake him from my head, like undoing an arrangement of the hair. (*For P, "him" is a side of himself.*)

-Paul C, *Partage de Midi* 42

P/R (*R is at an increasing distance.*) Keep this horrible mess well held together!

-Paul C, *P de M* 43

Clotho, 1893

-E Barrett
Browning on
George Sand
(CB22)

J   all unshorn, floats back dishevelled strength in agony.

-author re C C's
[*Clotho*]

A   The tossed head throws off the water, throws off the hair, throws off the blood.

P/C	I was the flesh that folded beneath you. Now see it unfolded!	-Paul C, *P de M* 149
A	unfleshed,	-RMP (2RMP135)
C	no legs, no arms, no teeth, no hair, only life enough to know her own horror.	-author
C/M	But horror is no deed. Touch me.	
P/C	(*C triumphantly, P desperately:*) That at least is mine. That broken thing is the work of the woman,	-P C, *P de M* 54 -P C, *P de M* 133
J	through this heavy thing on her head,	-J actor on [*Clotho*]
C	out of the head, this abstraction. (*To P:*) I will put a leaning tree which will express destiny.	-author -Camille C letter to Paul C (1RMP69)
M	(*Simultaneously with the first few next words of C's:*) But alone I have made what my sisters un-make, my hair, my life too long without my sisters…	-author
C	(*to M:*) But alone I have made what your sisters unmake, your hair your life too long without your sisters, one to hold it on the distaff and (*to R:*) one to cut it off. And at the banquet to which	-Bullfinch's *Mythology* on Clotho

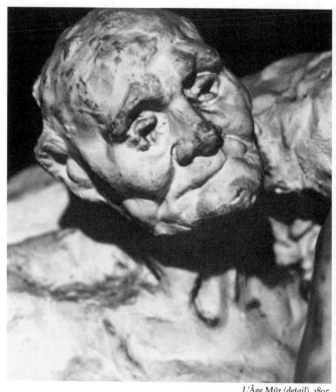

L'Âge Mûr (detail), 1895

-RMP (2RMP139)

-author

you can invite no woman, (*Somewhere in here
R gets congratulated as if he had made* Clotho.)
the men wished me to show her like this again.

(*referring to, then speaking to* M:) You discovered it over you, unwinding, blinding, binding, and through what, whose move, his wish? It will break the bone in your neck before it covers you. You are bellyless, hilarious. It is your batwing, your curtsy, your black sail, your leaning tree, your brain name, your commodity.

- ("Cerveaux" LC's maiden name = brains)

A He resists with his central pillar, but this first male nude by a woman is an outcast of the body, bald, beardless, stumbling, bent into exile.

-Paul C, *Ma Sœur Camille* on [*L'Âge Mûr*] (female like Clotho) (JC129)

P/M (*to R, P identifying with C:*) I hold you for good,

-RMP (2RMP) on [*L'Age Mûr*]
-Paul C, *L'A F à M* 76

A but really too determined a taste for ugliness, which is a little bit a caricature of his genius.

-Romain Rolland, contemp poet & critic (JC139) on [*L'Âge Mûr*]

P/M/C (*Continuing the line before last:*) your hand and the arm with it, and everything that comes with the arm.

-Paul C, *L'A F à M* 76

A His arm is parallel to her arm. The arm is exaggerated around the head, this shoulder tends to become that arm, Hermaphrodite misformed by the grasp of more complex age. And this other arm, whose hands grew from their other shoulders, has been cut apart, and these now other arms have the name of a dragged foot.

-author [*L'Âge Mûr*]

- ("Claudel" echoes claudiquer, "limp"; CC had a slight limp)

93

-Paul C, *Ma Sœur Camille* (JC134) on [*L'Âge Mûr*]	P	It's my sister, imploring, on her knees; see how this proud woman interprets herself. What is torn from her is all at once her soul, genius, reason, beauty, life, the name itself.
-JC (JC134) -author (drawing is comparable)	A	Her brother's comment leaves no ambiguity: we know this lover, and yet the skull in its one gesture away resembles a drawing of the father. (*The others look as if for the father, look finally at P, who, momentarily, in relation to M as mother, takes R's place in the trio.*)
-Louis Paul Claudel (father of Camille & Paul) (JC157) -P C, *L'A F à M*	P	(*Reading a letter from the father:*) "My son, it breaks my heart to leave her to her isolation." (*Then, as himself, as if to C:*) It's the house you are scorning, your patrimony you're rejecting!
-author	C	(*To R:*) Yes, you are, aren't you?
-P C, *L'A F à M* 76 -P C, *L'A F à M* 201	R/P	Parents, your daughter is no longer yours. It's mine alone! But this mouth, this mouth of your daughter, this mouth wasn't hers, it's mine!
-Cochard, contemp critic (JC89-90)	A	He was absent, but among his numerous imitators, her talent must be acknowledged.
-P C, *L'A F à M* 201	R/P	I say this mouth and the breath of life that's between the lips.

L'Implorante, 1905

C   I thought I had talked of speech but I had only   -author
spoken. And this is what I said. Being silenced
works. I can't talk of myself because you can't
talk. A thing is speakable, but has no intention,
because outside of you. I mean to want nothing, but I want to say so, so can't say what I mean.
I want to tell you but can say nothing, but that
telling, telling would pour open,

C/P   once, ten times, all the way.

-author   C   I need you to get rid. Rid of speech, rid of you, leaving you in abandon of the impossible hope of speech, of love as the possibility of breaking the absence of speech, of speech as the possibility of breaking the absence of love.

(*C turns away from R, who is already at a distance. He's not around for a while after this, and then only separate, or as an echo or projection. In fact all the characters more or less keep their distance in this scene from now on; they may form sculptural references, though in these they seem caught up in the imagination of them, whereas they regard her as an object of curiosity or fear. Even their sympathy is objective.*)

-PC, *P de M* 49   P   (*Who is up to his own thing, possibly writing.*) Wanting to be opened in the middle like a book and pronounced like a word on a voice.

-author   C   (*To R:*) You fed me your language mouth-to-mouth, but

-PC, *L'A F à M* 201   P/C   (*Shouting:*) I say this mouth and the breath of life between the lips!

P   (*Pulling himself together:*) The agitation of our family, their grain of madness. I have always had a distaste for mad people, passionate, excited people. The artistic vocation inspires literal terror in me from that point of view.

-PC, *Journal*

C   (*To P:*) You never talk to me about your writing.

-Camille C letter to Paul C (1RMP73)

P/C   I hear.

-PC, *L'A F à M* 157

P/C/J   (*J has been siding with M when not involved in the sculptural action.*) What do you hear?

P/C   I hear things existing with me.

A   The feeling of solitude she experiences is so great that she sometimes has the strange fear of forgetting the use of speech. And she talks aloud, to reassure herself.

-Morhardt essay *Mlle Camille Claudel* (JC431)

C   (*Still to P:*) You'll be quite thrilled if you get the idea, tiny little people around a huge table, listening, there, absent, absorbed in the thing, the table, the listening, the wall, a young girl crouching on a bench, crying, absent, there, her parents look at her in complete astonish-

-Camille C letter to Paul C (1RMP69-71) -author on the sketches she is refering to

Les Causeuses, 1897

-Camille C letter
to Paul C
(1RMP69-71)

-Morhardt Mlle
CC (JC432-3)

A

ment. You're the only person I'm confiding these ideas in. Don't show them!

At other times she looks from her window out onto the vast courtyard of miracles. A couple of street singers patiently look up to the closed

shutters for some little coin to drop on the re-
sounding pavement.

C   (*To P:*) So I'm asking you if it's not an inconve-
nience for you to send me 150 to 200 francs.

-Camille C letter to
Paul C
(1RMP69-71)

P   (*Ignoring the plea: writing, or to* A:) Everywhere,
sad men in clothes dirty their pedestals with a
green juice. And naked women continue to be
chiseled out for the graves of cemetery and mu-
seum. My sister is the first worker of an interior
sculpture.

-Paul C, *Camille
Claudel,
Sculpteur*
(1RMP13)

A   The idea of representing them naked already
transgresses reality and removes the scene from
time, but in a second time the artist overshad-
ows her tiny women with an immense wall and
places her speaking woman in a corner like an
oracle.

-RMP on Camille
C sculpture [*Les
Causeuses*]
(2RMP46)

C   I have never endowed my material with intention, but this is immaterial to my imagination.
This is not theory but happens when women
leave doors open while occupied with their
hands, and keep talking. I touch. What do you
touch? I don't touch pictures. I am moved when
reminded and reminded when I move that the
screen would be too small and the foot too large,

-author on
Camille C
sculpture [*Les
Causeuses*]

99

though still a thing, so fitting. The back of the screen is the back of the world, as the untouchable becomes a thing, and touchable, and you see your touch,

-A actor

C/P (*Whispering:*) do not touch,

-author on Camille C sculpture [*La Vague*]

C and my eyes flatten my palm on what is invisible. I am the tedious storm, reflected in the glassy scoop of my own erosion. I suck a great lump of soul outside of the bodies. We are protected by the jewel of mass. We are deep in a listening surge of place. I am after nature. I am the speaking woman. My charms crack not; and Time goes upright. You discovered me over and around you; I am your closed shutters, your mouth of salt, your green brute of a detail. And we imitate your abstraction,

-Shakespeare, *Tempest*

-author as above

-Paul C, *Ma Sœur Camille* (2RMP182)

P these two identical sisters whose hands I have already seized, with the right hand, and with the left hand, (*He does so.*) and who are none other than myself,

-(Paul C: CC used sheep bone to polish her sculpture, after Bernini)

C/P/J hypnotised in the hollow polished by her bone. (*P and J looking up, C looking at their hands.*)

La Vague, 1898

-Morhardt article (JC450)	A	She had to become a smith, and to hammer, bathe and sharpen herself the steels for the chisels, files and bores she used.
-Camille C letter to Paul C (JCl88)	C	A mouldmaker I couldn't pay immediately destroyed several finished pieces in my workplace.
-Morhardt letter to Paul C (JC187)	A	She has just spent a difficult week with two assistants that she sent away and who persecuted her quite maliciously. We have had them arrested. She is always having things stolen, money, which is one thing, but her time and work, which is everything.
-author	C	I hadn't forgotten that for a moment but remembered the not yet legal difference we are having here this is the porous site of, legal in the sense of, oh, just money. Every time I put a new grouping into circulation, millions roll for the foundries, the casters and the dealers. And for me, Zero plus zero equals zero. Last night two individuals tried to break in. Two of *his* Italian models. The sad old man gets all his work from me by different means, and shares them with his pals, who in exchange decorate him, give him ovations, banquets…

-Camille letter to Eugene Blot, friend & curator (1RMP82)

-Camille C letter to H Asselin

-Camille C letter to Paul C (1RMP114)

They deny me. They keep me for this. What -author does it give them? To take what they need and pretend it has only come from them. The more they need to think or say has come from them, the more they deny me. What they want is not me, but something in me that they want for themselves. They look at me and see, not their female self whose impossibility they want only to reach for eternally, to keep inside themselves, but my male self too, with which they compete, and with which they cannot co-exist, but which they envy and need to steal from. They imagine that not having their or my female self is love, when it is only impossibility, and they imagine that having my male self is merely themselves, when it is partial, and denial. And if they imagined that my male self is had by a female self, they would have to deny themselves what I can give of the power to know her. They must take her only themselves. This is rape. Rape because against the body, through the body, of the soul. They rape the man in the woman because they want the man of the woman, they want the woman without a man, and spit out the woman, without themselves.

-Paul C, *Mes Idées sur le Théâtre*	P	(*As a playwright/director's comment on the action:*) Often we are moved not so much by what the actor says as by what we feel he is about to say.
-Camille C letter to Morhardt (1RMP114) -author	C	(*Still about R:*) This famous man's ovations have cost me the eyes in my head, and for me, nothing…! Surely that's wrong. Use the following blank to figure this out. I forgot to mention his name, whoever he is, but you've all got one of your own, whoever you are.

end of scene 3
(*again continues temporally*)

SCENE FOUR

The first lines comment on the end of the last scene. As the debate ensues, there is a distinct public arena, like an exhibition; though C works alone, even if others walk around her like an object. C's area may be poorer and more original, with some contrast between her idea of it and others.' The audience can be included, perhaps by directing the lighting, in the exhibition, then at C's party.

C can no longer be self-absorbed artistically, but is struggling. No trust. Her language is often gleeful as earlier, but what previously was youthful power now sometimes deliriously contradicts appearances.

J is an acquaintance here. M is visible, increasingly resentful, and joins with a kind of triumph at the end.

A   Difficult, difficult, difficult, difficult, difficult, difficult, difficult. Then it really is better to be the Muse, or the assistant, or, I don't know, than to make the things yourself. Yes, I mean, art IS MASCULINE. Whether that's an advantage or a disadvantage for them, that really is the goddamm way we SEE it, the way we LIVE it. Seriously now blblbl… blblbl, and art quite clearly is masculine, that's er — THAT. IS. SO.   -A actor

107

-Henri Braisne, contemporary critic (JC) -RMP (1RMP67)		*(Having made the transition back into character:)* Still slim and beautiful when I visited her, in the photographs of her sculpting after the breakup, she has a heavy, mannish look,
-Camille C , quoted in Anne Delbée *Une Femme*	C	So this wretched art is better suited to old beards and ugly pears than to a woman relatively well endowed by nature?
-Henri Asselin, contemp critic (JC157) -Octave Mirbeau, contemp (1RMP21)	A	although the great dark eyes, shadowed, with black circles, had not yet lost their beauty. She is that revolt of nature, a female genius.
-Christine Battersby, *Gender & Genius* 26 (ref CB)	J	"Genius" in Latin refers to the forces associated with male fertility; "ingenium" is associated with knowledge and good judgement, also with talent. The words have been confused.
-Lavater, contemp (CB96) -David Hume [CB82] -Lavater (CB96)	A	Man observes; woman feels. Her hot passions must be tempered. Man is grave. *(The gradual or sudden contradictions may or may not be different personalities, or different books, though "endowed with intention" dramatically. Perhaps J could announce the sources.)*
-Camille C letter to Rodin (JC181)	C	I cannot go where you invite me as I have neither hat nor shoes, and my boots are quite worn out.

A   Women's works are as cold and pretty as women. The fire that emblazes and lights the soul is lacking in women's writing. They can be singers or dancers, interpreters. Laborious learning or painful pondering, even if a woman should greatly succeed in it, destroy the merits that are proper to her sex,

-JJRousseau (CB36)

-Ruskin (CB39)

-Kant (CB77)

P   a superb brow, rising above eyes of that blue so rarely found outside of novels. She is enormous, her face is dirty.

-Paul C *MSC* (JC391)
-Paul C, *Journal* (JC169)

A   When a woman has scholarly inclinations there is usually something wrong with her sexually. The only female genius is a man. The man of genius possesses the complete female in himself. An artist desires to win honor, power, wealth, fame and the love of women.

-Nietzsche (CB122)
-Goncourt (CB34)
-Weiniger (CB113)

-Freud (CB134)

C   I desperately need money to pay my rent for October, otherwise I'll be woken up one of these mornings by my usual bailiff, coming to get me with his usual delicacy.

-Camille C letter to Eugene Blot (JC181)

P   I believe her to be, apart from the small liking I have for her, a woman of genius.

-Paul C letter (JC160)

J   She is the complete figure of the female ge-

-Gabrielle Reval,

contemp female critic(JC152)		nius, two magnificent eyes of a pale green evocative of young shoots in the forest.
-Paul C, *Journal* (JC169)	P	She speaks incessantly in a monotonous, metallic voice.
-Lacan (paraphrase)	A	Language is the masculine domain of the symbolic order. It is anxious, it differentiates. The real is not self, it is proximity to female orgasm, the undifferentiating, the other.
-author -C actor	C	I am not the other, I am not unnameable. I am [NAME OF C ACTOR]. I hate it when people are doing something, and I'm there, and they think they're geniuses, and I notice it. I've perceived this trait in, almost always in men. When something important comes from a woman, I believe that she has a hard time finding a man who's prepared to feel himself, next to her work, nevertheless taken seriously as part of her life. My mother is alone because she made the choice to follow seriously her own things that are right for her, and because all the men she met, who didn't have a lot to do with influencing how she did it, always felt themselves to be in the weaker position, and so they couldn't have got involved with my mother, they couldn't get involved.

P   The character to whom the poet is trying to give life, speech and movement is not entirely the child of his own thought.   -Paul C, *Mes Idées sur le Théâtre*

A   (*Not paying attention:*) How much of the artist have *I made*, in that I've criticized him? Well, also this, sticking to what has been the Muse, I *lead* a, an artist and I advise him, I bring him themes…   -A actor

C   I heard some music very recently. I found it genius. Whether the people who played it are all geniuses, is of no interest. Genius is PR, it's macho, meaning egotistic and exclusive, unable to differentiate from their own viewpoint. It's a reason for a lot of brutality, it's old-fashioned, it's the biography, not the work. It's not useful. Talk instead about foresight, both penetration and encompassment. The work. In the world. Excitement. The greatest talent is to make something of your talent. I expect craft from people I work with. Talk of genius avoids multiple respect for creativity. It suggests the inhuman. (*First hint of Perseus and the Gorgon figures.*) I can't… finish… this sentence.   -C actor   -author   -C actor   -author   -C actor

A   She was shaking a duster out of the window, although it was three in the afternoon, and in a   -H Asselin (JC400)

rather hoarse voice, singing some frou-frou of the time. She stared me out suspiciously.

-Paul C, *Mes Idées sur le Théâtre*   P   One voice was not enough for the poet. He had to have that group working together on the stage.

-Carol Wheeler (song on album UK Blak)   C/J   You said you'd never turn your back on anyone. Success brought us to the top of the ladder. But you turned saying, don't come any closer. This is mine, don't come any closer. This is mine, etc. (*Should be sung gradually with joy like a song.*)

-author - Camille C sculpture of own head with fruit   C   I was allowed to *make* fruit on my head because this is a figure. This is a figure because the material is untrue but we know the colors of grapes and apples.

-H Asselin (JC403-404)   A/P/M   She was not known to have any friends; and then, one fine evening, the day after she received some unexpected money, the ground floor would suddenly fill with a crowd of unknowns popping champagne all night long.

(*C, J and the audience are at the party, but don't let them get too excited.*)

A For these horrifying parties, among the marbles, the maquettes draped with wet cloth, in an apartment of unbelievable bareness, she, who had dressed up, sported the most outrageous frocks and above all hairstyles made of ribbons and feathers combining the loudest and least harmonious colors. For there was in this artist of genius something forever childlike, an excess, a clash, an absence of taste, which only the beauty of her work and the niceness of her intentions could allow one to forgive.

-H Asselin, as above

C (*Party over—gets angry*:) You have stripped me of my dress of speech. I was not allowed to *wear* fruit on my head, because although the words have allowed me to come back I have not been myself while here, although, my mouth to a preferred mouth, it has taken me most of myself. (*The scene darkens*).

-Aeschylus, *Agamemnon* (Cassandra) -author

A I myself was in the depths of Szechuan. Her brother had gone back to China.

-H Asselin, as above

P The professional absentee, whose fate, whose very condition of existence is no longer to have a hold on anything but the single thread that carries him from one place to another. (*He has*

-Paul C, *L'Absent Professionel* Cahiers 4

Buste de Paul Claudel à 42 ans, 1910

at last more or less achieved a separate identity,
through official work and self-absorption.)

C   (*Destruction leading to construction—reminis-*
cent of the wall at the end of the Parodos, also
like a chimney corner (for next scene.) An object
does not speak, but can be apprehended, because outside of you. My feet are huge, my
hands are huge, and I swallow the world. My
arms surround, and I am a curl of the world.

-author

| | The muscles insinuate through me the pleasure | -Paul C, *Mémoires Improvisées* |

The muscles insinuate through me the pleasure
of messing in the middle of the matter.

-Paul C,
*Mémoires
Improvisées*

C/A   Thou earth, thou, speak!

-Shakespeare,
Tempest

C   She is

J/A   (*And C's voice fading as she works*:)
a place chill below Atlas lying,
of solid to be guardianed with armament of mass,
whose in entrance twin inhabited sisters
daughters of Phorcys, single shared of eye the use.
That Perseus with skills furtively while passed, slyly
with put-in stole with hand.
And through said away long
and path away, and of woodland bristling boul-
    ders of broken,
of Gorgons gained to home. And throughout
    through fields
and through ways had seen of men simulacra
    and of beasts,
into stone out of self of sight changed of Medusa.
He but of horror in shield which on left wore
in bronze rebounding shape observed of
        Medusa,
and while heavy sleep and snakes and herself
    was holding,
sliced head from neck.

-Ovid
Metamorphoses
(Perseus & the
Gorgon)

-Paul C, *MSC*, on Camille C sculpture [*Perseus et la Gorgone*] (2RMP198)	P	What is this head of bloody hair but an image of madness? This face at the end of the raised arm, yes, I think I recognize its disturbed features.
		(The characters of the sculpture/story correspond to those in the Parodos. C of course is the Gorgon, a tragic one, swept aside by time.)
-H Asselin (2RMP198)	A	with all the vulgarity of a kind of harridan.
-Morhardt paraphrase of CC (JC441,1RMP315)	C/A	In what has been you must only keep what is necessary to explain what will be.
-author (R sculpture *L'Homme au Nez Cassé*)	C	Let's break something. A nose? Can be sexy, on a man.
-Debussy	A	I see her, shocking herself, breaking everything, breaking herself.
-Paul C, *Violaine* (1RMP38)	P	I have seen her walking, the violent woman.
-Louis P C, Camille C's father, letter to Paul C (JC171)		*(Reading letter from father:)* I would like her to come to see us from time to time. Your mother won't hear of it, but I wonder if it wouldn't be a way of calming, if not curing, her rage. If you take care of her, I am deeply grateful.

	(Placing him in the past already:) My father was a kind of mountain man, nervous, temperamental, imaginative to a fault, ironic, bitter.	-Paul C letter (JC39)
C/P	*(P writing:)* The oriole whistles in the middle of the pink and golden tree. What does he say? That it's time for the old man to go away and leave the world to its business.	-Paul C, *L'A F à M* 78
P	*(As writer/director, in contrast to C who reacts to the realization of the loss of her father by going wild, inside the moment:)* I want a proper door that will open. He opens both sides when the oriole sings. With a little shiver on "saaay."	-Paul C, *Mes Idées sur le Théâtre*
C	See there! See there!	-Aeschylus, *Agamemnon* (Cassandra)
P	*(Writing a religious line:)* Pax! pax! pax!	-Paul C, *L'A F à M*
C/P	*(P continuing, C in grief:)* Father! father! father!	
C	I was so angry that I took all my wax sketches and flung them into the fire, it gave me a beautiful blaze, and I warmed my feet in the glow of the flames. That's what I do when something unpleasant happens to me, I take my hammer and I smash a man. The big statue shortly followed the fate of his little wax sisters, *(The de-*	-Camille C Letter (BFPellerin bio)

117

struction increasingly amplifies the gesture of "pounding to dust" of the "child" in Scene Two.)

-Paul C, *Violaine* (1RMP38)	C/P	against the hurricane that folds back her wings!

-Ovid *Metamorphoses* (Atlas)	A/J	for beard and hair

                     into woods went away, ridges were and
                            shoulders and arms,
                     what head before was, peak was on mountain
                            top,
                     bones stone became; parts in all
                     grew to unmeasure, and whole
                     with all stars sky rested on him.

(C's constructions are crashed down to form a mountain or walls for the next scene.)

-PC, *On Racine* re Cassandra in Aeschylus' *Agamemnon*	P	A certain limit is reached. The excess of a distraught heart has broken the borders of the two worlds.

-author	C	Fathers and daughters strewn straight up, you must believe us, heading for the eye of the storm, not down with the ship in the throat of its own eye, on the tremendous peninsula the wreck of the relation,

P   Daughter, know your father.   -PC, *L'A F à M* 74

C/A   childless, she sank   -Ovid (Niobe),
       amid corpses of sons and daughters and hus-   [*La Niobide*
          band,   *Blessée*] Camille
       and grief made her stone.   C sculpture

P   But the father sees his children outside of him-   -Paul C, *L'A F à M*
       self and knows what was entrusted in him.   73-4

(M & P lift her, though she doesn't really change atti-
tude, so they just shift her from a position embracing
the stone, such as La Niobide Blessée part of
Sakountala, with stone instead of the male, or one of
the Cheminées, to a position that continues the sculp-   -[*La Cheminée*]
tures that R has represented her as/in: that is, increas-   CC sculptures
ingly trapped in or part of the stone.)

C/A   Not one hair stirs in the breeze;   -Ovid (Niobe)
       her face is bloodless; her eyes stare immobile;
       this image does not live; her tongue congeals
       to silence against her palate, and her veins
          stop unable;
       she can not move her neck to flex nor arms to
          reach
       nor feet to go; the organs inside her are rock.
       But she is crying. And spun in a gusting
          whirlwind force,

she is rapt away to her father's land;
where it pours from her fixed on the
  mountain peak.
Tears seep from the marble still.

(end of scene 4)

SCENE FIVE

C doesn't move in this whole scene. Stark lighting, maybe along the floor to give distance.

During the course of the previous scene, one of the structures made and destroyed, but not totally rendered unrecognizable, is a fireplace. Now M sits here. It separates her from C. Everyone else is further away (they can be doing their things, distantly), but J and P approach gingerly, only J touching her.

A's repetitive comments, in contrast to the next scene, are a distant echo or bass line, not interrupting the flow of the monologue or correspondences.

Disillusion and acting. Surface. The body's rule. C's retreat into the voice, embedding parts of her earlier history.

C   The giantess has a man's name. In one of her   -author
      hands is her sheer face, the mouth of hole a
      rocked door in her walls higher than a woman's
      head of loneliness. She is a place. With his other
      hellish hand, he is the lump his age caresses, as
      once, that took stone's moment, stole, stormed
      and stormed a grain from her lost lip.

123

-C C's doctor (1RMP193) as all A's dated Dr. lines

A   1913 March 7: I certify that she has serious intellectual problems.

-Paul C, *L'A F à M* 150

C/P   Hey, no-face! Hey, the eaten one!

-Paul C, *L'A F à M* 22

C/P/R   But we left the little teeth like seeds below the great founding block.

-author

C   I am the tedious storm, reflected in the glassy scoop of my own erosion.

A   1913 March 8: I certify that the so named suffers from a systematic delirium of persecution, based principally on interpretations and fabulations: she has the idea of being the victim of criminal attacks by a famous sculptor, who has got hold of her masterpieces and wishes to poison her; she also shut herself in her home.

-A actor

       (*As actor:*) And the same story, mhp, mhp, the very similar story… goes for the, for the doctor, for the, who's also an analyst like the critic, yes, also. He's always in the permanent dilemma, er, to choose.

-Paul C, *L'A F à M* 17

C/P   Doormaker, let me open this one for you.

A   1913 April: idem.

C/P   Then raise this veil.   -Paul C, *L'A F à M*
                                                    157

A   1913 May: same state, calm.

C/P   Below that one I have another.

A   1913 June: idem.

C/P   Can you no longer see?

A   1913 August: idem.

C/P   I no longer have eyes.

A   1913 September: idem.

C/P   I hear.

A   1913 October: no change.

C/P   What do you hear?

A   1913 November: idem.

C/P   I hear things existing with me.

A   1913 December: idem.

-Louise C letter to Dr. (1RMP126)	M	Other than to myself and to her brother, I formally forbid that she write to anyone whatsoever and that she receive any communication, visit or letter from whoever there might be.
-author	C	Objects do not fall from the world in spontaneous season.
-A actor	A	1914 February: same state. Well, quite simply the doctor's jealousy of the artist... the jealousy then of not being like that himself, so direct and so extreme and so er...
-Ovid, *Metamorphoses* [Gorgon]	C/A	Sliced head from neck.
	A	1914 March: same state.
-contemporary newspaper article (JC206)	J	It's up to him (*P*) to put an end to the odious imprisonment that has already lasted only too long and which has all the signs of revenge.
-Paul C, *Journal*	P	Very well. I have received so much undeserved praise that calumnies are good and refreshing. It's the Christian's lot.
-author (see Scene One)	C	Woman has no arms or head. I have made these my work.

A 1914 April: same state.

C/P Do I have fifty souls to tear out of my own? -Paul C, *L'A F à M* 169

A 1914 May: same state.

C This is not a body in simple relation to itself. These are the parts of a body that almost cannot hold itself, on the chisel-edge of what almost cannot hold itself, the weight of the blank of the world. -author

A 1914 July: same state.

C And now we are later, just, and held, just.

A 1914 August: same state.

C Some man or other must present wall. -Shakespeare, *A Midsummer Night's Dream*

A 1914 September: false interpretations and imaginations.

C And let him hold his fingers, thus.

A 1914 October: Needs shoes.

M She must not be able to pass letters out secretly. -Louise C letter to Dr. (1RMP128)

127

-author

C   We read with our bodies the things that are place, and now we are here, just, and we are also, just.

A   1914 November: idem.

-author

C   Slippage, upturn, danger, scoop. No fall. No crime. No corpse.

(J makes as if to enter C's space, but is restrained by A, not as a rule, but that it's not her business.)

A   1914 December: idem.

-Maria Paillette (childhood friend of C, still knows mother) (1RMP129)

J   But it isn't a crime to want to live alone and to love one's cats. If it was, half the village would be shut up!

-Camille C letter to her cousin (1RMP129)

C   You know how much I've suffered being separated from my dear work.

A   1915 April: well physically.

-Paul C letter to an acquaintance (2RMP282)

P   *(To someone else:)* Someone very close to me committed the same crime as you, and she lives her days out in a lunatic asylum. To kill a child! Tolerance? There are houses for that.

-Paul C to another acquaintance

C   How is it that since then you haven't written to me once and never came back to see me?

-Camille C letter to Paul C (1RMP130)

A   1915 September: still well.

C   Are you be do yes no? Once there were three pears. They are still there. Here we go again, scratching in the happy ending in the light of, say, love, mine or someone else's. Or maybe the smell of lavender through the snow, or using "usual" without judging, but after all this time I'm new to this and have never seen fog and snow together before, which is why I have allowed hatchings to grow on my hand in order that they fill with calcium, after all, and may reach the end before me and pulse back dim signals indistinguishable from habit from here. If you can't leave your body you might as well leave it the privilege, levering the permanent spring from ankle to hair.

-author

M   She asks me to take her immediately back to my home. It's not possible. I'll never agree to this arrangement. She gave us the runaround just too long. She complains that her letters are not sent to the friends who would come and get her out if they knew how unhappy she is. It was very wrong of you to tell her that it was I

-Louise C letter to Dr.(1RMP132)

who said she should not receive news from anyone. I ask for your support in making her understand that she stays with you.

A   1915 October: same mental state, wants to make her own food, doesn't want to stay here, wants to go back to Paris, etc.

-PC, *Tête d'Or* 241

C/P   When I left your country I was chased to here.

-PC, *T d'O* 165-6

P/C   I'm cold. I'm hungry. Will this terrible night never end? What do the trees say that know everything? They protest endlessly, like men attached by the leg. I came to this desert place, to this end of the earth, covering my body with leaves and the skins of animals, running from men like an animal, for fear they'll kill me or take me. And now I can no longer move from weakness and I must stay where I am! Wretched thing, how I wanted the sun, when he'll only uncover me to everyone! But when I try to rush towards evil, may it be with a limp in my foot! and I lie like a kid with a broken hoof, at the mercy of those who pass. Long pause. Sunrise. I'm cold. I'm hungry.

-Paul C, *Journal*

-Paul C, *T d'O* 165-6

-Louise C letter to Dr. (1RMP 133)

M   As for taking her with me or letting her go back where she was, never, never, never. Keep her, I beg you. She spent her time writing letters to nobodies or making denunciations. She has every vice, I no longer want to see her again, she hurt us too much. I beg you again to find out through whom she is passing letters.

P   The moment has not yet come for me to let go of whatever it may be that I am attached to. To compromise by any attempt at thought the solidity of the precarious barrier that defends me against the future.

-Paul C, *La Rose et le Rosaire*

A   1917 1st July, monthly report: Sometimes washes her food and takes minute precautions against poisoning.

C/P   This mouth you had given me.

-Paul C, *L'A F à M*
120

C/P   (*P writing, almost relishing:*) Hard to know you'll never recover and nothing can be done for it, and to be alone and to bear your own poison, and to feel yourself decay alive! And not death, only savoring it, once, ten times, but losing none of it, all the way. And here you are turning to me with this smile full of poison.

-Paul C, *L'A F à M*
131-3

C   I am not an image.

-Paul C, *L'A F à M*

-Paul C (1RMP317)	P	All loved ones are vessels of gall drunk with the eyes closed.
-Louise C letter to Camille C (1RMP131-3)	M	(*To C:*) How dare you accuse me of poisoning your father? Your letter is a collection of insults, each one more hateful than the last. But you don't say if you got the coat or the coffee and biscuits. Of course, that doesn't count.
-Camille C letter to a former co-inmate (1RMP134)	C	Maman doesn't admit it but she's not happy! When I think how poor Papa already died without my knowing it, and he called for his daughter, his daughter! and his daughter didn't come!
-Paul C, *L'A F à M* as above	C/P	This mouth you had given me, this daughter you had given me.
	A	1919 June: Not in a state to get out and manage her fortune.
-author -Camille C letter to Louise C (1RMP140)	C	I will not eat my words, though they refuse to fall from my lips. It's so cold I could no longer stand up. I am forced to go to my room on the second floor where it's so freezing that I have chilblains, my fingers are shaking and can't hold the pen.

A   1919 December: Calm, but has the same sick ideas. Asks to see her family and would like to be closer to them.

M   She asks to have a paraffin lamp but probably you won't allow her.

-Louise C letter to Dr. (1RMP135)

C/A   The rooms and corridors are not heated, the rules forbid it.

-M Morhardt (critic sympathetic to CC) letter to PC (JC)

C   I did not get warm all winter, I am frozen to the bone, cut in two by the cold. Nothing can give you the idea of the cold of here. And it lasts seven months in all.

-CC letter to Louise C (1RMP141)

C/J   Cold dwells there, and Fear and Shuddering, and Famine. Go and tell the last to take possession of the bowels.

-Ovid, *Metamorphoses* (tr Bullfinch) Hunger, a female, cf [*Clotho*]

C   The women have dysentery from one end of the year to the next, an old beef stew, black, oily and bitter, from one end of the year to the next, an old dish of macaroni swimming in slime, and for dessert three horny old figs.

-Camille C letter to Louise C (1RMP141)

A   1920 3 January: Eats to her taste. Manifests a desire to see you.

-CC letter to Louise
C (1RMP141)   C   The coffee is chickpea water.

-Ovid as above   C/J   And he strove to nourish his body by eating his body, till death relieved him.

A   1920 1 May: Weakened interpretations, though not completely disappeared. Shows a strong desire to go back to her family and to live in the country. I think that under the circumstances, this could be tried.

-Louise C, letter
to Dr. (1RMP137)   M   From the letters I receive, her ideas haven't changed at all. She continues to treat us as thieves who let her enemies into her workplace full of works of art, and having thrown her cases in the rubbish, among which was a bust of Victor Hugo, etc, while in fact these cases contained nothing but unformed packets of clay, which we had a hard time getting rid of. It's impossible to believe that she has a healthy mind, no more now than when we put her into your establishment because we couldn't stand her incoherences.

A   1920 June: The weakening of her ideas of persecution could allow a trial release.

M   You can't let persecuted people out without great danger, because as soon as they're at home, they quickly get their ideas back. I can not authorize you to try letting her out.

-Louise C, letter to Dr. (1RMP137)

C/P   What did I repeat in my silence?

-Paul C, T d'O 21

A   1920 July: If you cannot take her back, you could place her in a home closer to her family, which could occasionally come to visit her. This absence of visit is very hard on her.

C   I am not what I mean, or I may be. The world is not what it intends. No one knows any longer what I see. How can this be silence when they try to stop my voice? If this may be what any interpret, why be? How? (*Then, trying to seem normal, though knowingly:*) Dear Maman, I received today your wonderful package. All the articles are excellent, I am always well served although I am far. I wouldn't make any scandal. I'd be too happy to come back to normal life. I wouldn't dare to move, I've suffered so much. I kiss you, thanking you heartily for your superb gift.

-author

-Camille C letter to Louise C (1RMP144)

-as above (1RMP142)

-as above (1RMP144)

C/P   (*She is desperate, he is denying.*) Gift of death, door of death, go enrich another than me.

-Aeschylus, Agamemnon (quoted in Paul C On Racine)

135

-Louise C, letter to Dr. (1RMP138)

M   I don't know any establishment as cheap as yours, and my resources are limited to the amount I currently give, it's impossible for me to give any more.

A   1920 September: Believes her mother under the influence of her friends, and thinks this to be the reason she has left her shut up.

-Camille C letter to Paul C (1RMP145-7)

C   (*Still trying to act normal:*) My dear brother, You make great sacrifices for me. You must have a solid head to govern things with so much intelligence. But in a madhouse changes are rather difficult to make. It's all shouting, singing and screaming, violent, strident and threatening. It laughs and sobs and tells endless stories. You must get me out of this place after all the years shut up. This money you spend on me I could use to make beautiful works. For all those millionaires even my poor workplace excited their envy! They said, we'll use a madwoman to find our subjects. Not even the right to have a home! I would like to close my own door. I would like so much to be at the chimney corner at home. While mother was alive I constantly implored her to get me out, but I came up against a wall. He's got you all in his game, without your realizing.

-CC letter to Louise C (1RMP149)

-cf [*La Cheminée*] CC sculpture -CC letter to PC (1RMP150)

P Passable. But we need a real door. We can do without the saints.

-Paul C, *Mes Idées sur le Théâtre*

A/P (*Reading:*) She remains persuaded that mother was poisoned.

-Louise C (sister) letter to Paul C

A 1921 April: A few false interpretations remain, limited to thinking she is the victim of revenge or of a mistake.

C I have been trying to keep my own voice out of this, knowing that it offers my own ear an un- fair counterpoint, like the snake who doesn't die of his own poison. If I were to speak how I could therefore think, this would also be con- sidered so gross exaggeration and stamped in the bottom left corner by a young man earnest with ambition while I was drunk at a party told to you, or will be, you'll see, as evidence against my authenticity, unlike his own gullibility in which he can rejoice, singing signed, signed be in chemicals till I turn her picture away, which noise stops the noise though not how I don't understand how what he wants inheres in here, and in here. Was he paid, by whom, how much, in what? Need I interpret green, grey, white, cream, gold, bronze, brass, bluegreen, fleshgreen? Chroma enact. Anyway imitates. It

-author

137

-Aeschylus,
Agamemnon
(Cassandra)

-[*Les Causeuses*]

comes when it comes. I open the door and put my hand in, neither afraid that nor pretending that this is a person, except maybe a photo on a dust jacket, or sleeve, imitated by my hand, I notice when I take it out again. I have made a chink to the back of the world. Of course, looking through the chink, you still can't see the back, because it faces the other way. And she, or I, turned to face this way, know the chink at my back, whether or not the wall looks like the world. She holds on her lap her work towards and so from possibility, and I don't, and her relation to her back and so to me is possibility, and mine is not. My being invited to begin from the world, and why indeed take away the lucky number you first stood on, laughs at me in my own language, or accent, or voice, ha ha.

(*J approaches.*)

-Camille C letter
to art school
friend, Jessie
Lipscomb,
(2RMP273)

-Camille C letter
to Paul C
(1RMP149)

How amazing if it was true that you're getting ready to come to see me! It'll be such great joy for me, it seems impossible. I'm sending you a photograph of the local architecture, you'll have much to study as an artist. I kiss you from my heart. (*J has entered, reunion with Camille, though weak.*) Not one of my relatives has done so much. (*J sits a while.*)

138

Again the inorganic anonymous letter contains its desire, its biography, denying the abstraction of the wave and the fistprints of the giantess, but the fingerprints of the giantess are as delicate as our eyes need to squirm on her nauseous edge of our own terrible abstraction, or rather, a sickening example of something she had never heard of. The promise solidifies its infidelity. We are anachronisms in timelessness. What a relief, that is, I cannot go where you say as I have no hat, or shoes, my boots are all worn out, that is, I will attend but will be unable to come as myself, or herself, or above all yourself who I hope will at least explain to him (*He or him is always R.*) that it is not only in her dream that he will be unable to appear as the equivalent he expects to approach any more than the word symbolic can be believed to appear innocently in the vicinity of a symbol or you to have figured out that the pears have now frozen, no, but here in his mouth where the stone hits. I am relying here on many weaknesses taking their course, particularly since only I interpret them as such. I'm not talking taste here, just some kind of worm in the mineral of modernity, found there or put there and wired for electricity. Did we get out of that one? He (*still R*) should get out of everything, since I am no

-author

-Camille C card to Rodin before her internment (JC181)

-author

-("worm" =flaw in sculptor's marble-Morhardt JC449)

longer speaking to him, and let it, it being everything, drop the dripping finger so that I can tell the back from the front of the thing, if any, let the solid be an emotional comment, and the emotional a thing.

-(some of the [*Cheminées*] had a tiny electric lamp which RMP considers kitsch)

A   1922 August: Doesn't think we wish to poison her.

C   At this point an impression of a memory of horror apparently concomitant with making, calling it existing, suspends not only better judgement but its ghost from the hook in the ceiling, and with it the ceiling, making the midnight news next day, report's function being to dispel impressions by confirming its own evanescence and eat it too. Relief is reported as a happy mortality, and defines the springstones of chasms that failing springstones would invite dwelling on the bargain basement. And let this cold represent cold, which is also in everything, in this Night of which I am only one daughter, my black flag.

-[Clotho] was one of the Fates, daughters of Night

I can look again at what I see only if I see it as the same. I am not allowed to change this tyranny of things, so I can look again at what I see only if I see it as different. How can I try to protect myself from enclosure? I am what changes but what I can't see as my body hurries to detach itself inwards.

P   thin, yellow, old, old, old, her mouth furnished with a few awful stumps, no more than the skull, among indifference, I'm ashamed of my opulence, but she wants to live in the cheapest section.

-Paul C, *Journal* (2RMP282-3)

-Paul C as above (2RMP279)
-Paul C as above (2RMP283)

C   (*to P:*) bellyless, hilarious. Let's talk about your God who lets an innocent woman rot.

-author
-CC letter PC (1RMP151)

P   My voice reached her.

-Paul C, *Journal* (2RMP279)

A   1923 June: Mentally stationary.

C   I can't move from here, so refuse the solidity of here. I am far from what I touch, trying to be at least matter in the middle of the pliant matter of myself. And what had been surface and what had been immobile became a muscle of motive, parts of the body scratched out, parts of speech wetted on, down in the science of severance embedding completion as if emerging? Marked thing. What jerks and ekes me through the hour-years is this arguing of the body between the phenomenal of the world and its

-author

equivalence, loving the first to be alive, made, surprised or making, and needing the second to bear it, brunt or witness. It is in and by gesture that matter resembles other matter, that my voice resembles your gesture, and in re-sembles by, and resembles a pivot or leash or brute or ply, as with questions, such as whether I like it, or am her.

(end of Scene 5)

Camille Claudel, circa 1935

EXODOS

QUOTED FROM
(SOURCES IN
BRACKETS)

Only the area where C is remains lit. Again there is no obvious distinction between the previous scene and this, although C hardly speaks again.

During the scene, the other actors (R & M, J and finally P) gradually remove from the acting area (or into the audience), drop character, remove costume). As such (shown by "?") they join in unison in the repetitive verdicts, that is, in saying "Same mental state," or "Lost," or their paraphrases. Each could leave on his or her last line about disappearance.

This scene should go very fast. P is just catching up.

J   1876–77: David and Goliath

-(1RMP154) & all
lost work refs
following

?   Fallen into dust.

A   1923 November: Very bored. Says she is far from
        her family and would like to be closer. Her de-
        lirious ideas are weaker and she seems no longer
        likely to be violent or dangerous, might it not
        be possible to some extent to satisfy her?

-(1RMP202) & all
Dr. refs following

J   1881: Her brother at 13. Plaster.

147

?	Disappeared to this date.
A	1924 October: Seldom visited at present. Insistently requests to leave. Disappointed to have no family visit in a year.
J	1884: Bust of her father.
?	Disappeared to this date.
P	Death, our precious patrimony.
A	1925 January: No notable change. Docile.
J	1884: Portrait of her mother. Oil.
?	Destroyed.
A	1927 August: A visit would have no effect, favorable or otherwise, on her delirium, but would make our patient very happy.
J	1885: Study of a hand. Plaster.
?	Disappeared to this date.
A	1929 January: Certificate of situation for lawyer:

-Paul C, *L'Art Poétique*

Systematic delirium of persecution on the basis of false interpretations.

J   1885: Giganti. Plaster.

?   Disappeared to this date.

A   1930 January to December:

?   idem.

J   1888: Bust of Rodin. Terracotta.

?   Disappeared to this date.

A   1931 January to December:

?   Same situation.

A   I had lost all trace of you. It is not forgotten that in the scheming world of sculpture you and a few others brought authenticity. How could you deprive us of so much beauty? He (R) stopped in front of the portrait and cried. Time will put everything back in place. Take the hand I hold out to you.

-Eugene Blot
letter to Camille
C (ref to Rodin)
(1RMP151-2)

	J	1889: Charles L'Hermitte as a child. Plaster.
	?	Disappeared to this date.
-Paul C, *Connaissance du* *Temps*	P	Time is the means offered to all that will be in order that it no longer be.
	A	1932 January to December:
	?	Same situation.
	J	1889: Prayer. Plaster.
	?	Disappeared to this date.
	A	1933 January to December:
	?	No change.
	J	1892: The Waltz. First version. Plaster.
	?	Disappeared to this date.
	A	1934 January to December:
	?	Same mental state.

J   1892: The Waltz. Marble. Planned as a State commission.

?   Never made.

A   1935 January to December:

?   Same mental state.

J   1892: The Waltz. Bronze.

?   Disappeared to this date.

A   1936 January to December:

?   Same mental state.

J   1893: Clotho. Marble. Commissioned for the Musée du Luxembourg.

?   Now disappeared, in spite of considerable research. Rodin was keeping it to present at the appropriate time.

A   1937 January to December:

?   Same mental state.

A   1938

-Camille C letter to Paul C (1RMP152-3)

C   They'd like to force me to make sculpture here, and when I don't they give me all kinds of bother. At this time of year I think of our dear mother. I never saw her again since the day you took that deadly decision to send me to mental asylums. I think of this beautiful portrait I made of her in the shade of our beautiful garden. Her large eyes where you could read a secret pain, the spirit of resignation on her whole face, her hands crossed on her knees in complete abnegation: modesty, the feeling of duty pushed to excess, that was our mother. I don't think the hateful person I've often mentioned would dare to attribute it to himself, like the rest of my work, that would be too much, my mother's portrait.

(C slowly and momentarily takes on her description of the mother's pose, which looks like the pose in her own last photograph.)

-Paul C, *La Sequestrée* in *Seigneur, apprenez-nous à prier* (1RMP341)

P   (To *himself*:) Your soul that you believed was off rented out somewhere, you do know, don't you, that she had never left you? She was there, in that cell reached down that dark corridor with occasional windows, the present at the bottom of all this past.

J   1894: L'Implorante. Plaster. Has not been found.

A   1938 January to December:

P   That forgotten sister, our soul, to whom we were unfaithful.   -Paul C as above

?   Same mental state.

J   1895: L'Âge Mûr. Plaster. The second project definitively accepted by the State and never received.

?   It has disappeared to this date.

C   Well, I must go in now.   -Aeschylus, *Agamemnon* (Cassandra)

A   1939 January to December:

P   The imprisoned one has come out! Out of those wild and tearing cloths and wraps. No longer a madwoman, but our soul itself, without wrinkle or stain, it's the holy virgin!   -Paul C, *La Sequestrée est Sortie* in above

?   Same mental state.

J   1895: L'Âge Mûr. Bronze. The text of commission by the State was prepared

?   then annulled.

A   1940 January to December:

-Paul C, *L'Esprit et L'Eau*   P   Now I can see the key that frees, and it is not the one that opens but the one that closes!

?   Same mental state.

J   1897: Hamadryad. Marble and bronze.

?   This bust has today disappeared.

A   1941 January:

C   wrote recently.

J   1897: The Wave. Plaster.

?   Disappeared to this date,

J   it seems to have been… sold to Rodin.

A   1942 August: Mental state slightly worsened by the progressive establishment of a state of intellectual weakness currently predominant. Physical state shows weakening since the restrictions which are hard for psychopaths.

154

J   1898: Perseus and the Gorgon. Bronzes. 25 examples,

P   His left hand holds a mirror, and with his right arm, buckling in surprise and horror, he raises behind him the head of the Gorgon, where he cannot but recognize his own features. An image of remorse

-Paul C, *Journal*

-Paul C, *MSC*
(JC399)

?   of which none can be located at this date.

(*P leaves.*)

A   1943 January to April: Without change.

J   1900: La Fortune. Plaster. Disappeared to this date.

A   1943 May:

?   mediocre.

J   1905: The Flute Player. Plaster. Disappeared to this date.

A   1943 June to August:

	?	same situation.
	J	1910: Bust of her brother at 42. Plaster.
	?	Disappeared to this date.
	A	1943 September:
	?	Able to recognize, looks forward to your visit.
-Director of asylum in letter to Paul C's son years after Camille C's death (JC314-5)	A	1962 Dear Sir, In answer to your letter in which you express the desire to transfer the mortal remains of your aunt, buried on the 21 of October 1943, to the family vault, I regret to inform you that the land in question has been reused for the needs of the establishment, the information concerning the family of the deceased not having been provided to the cemetery administration.

(*The stones of her wall/mountain are removed as the problems of giving her a grave are recounted.*)

(*end of Exodos*)

EPILOGUE

This last scene, segueing from the Exodos, plays the role of history, and can lead from the play out to comment by actors and audience, as the prologue led in at the beginning, but now the audience's role as also interpreters should be clearer.

The actors give a few blunt comments, in their role or as themselves, on C, on interpretation, on the performance, but addressed in more conversational tones to the audience. This is not an attempt to start a discussion, though if the audience starts to, let them but lead them to do it among themselves, and extract yourself.

Some of the actors who have been less present towards the end could already be washed and modern, or partly, in contrast to C's dustiness.

end of play

TEXT AND STAGING DETAILS

The play's structure reflects its title. There is not only a single reality.

At the center of this delirium of interpretations, really only C, of all the roles, has her own subjective or invented voice. The rest of the characters, and C at times, speak through voices borrowed from history, even if these are manipulated. These range (not proportionately, since time has not bequeathed them so) from personal writings through artistic creations to critical comment; they also include other existing texts which have seemed appropriate, either as light on the background of individuals, or as reflective of climates of thought which have given or still give context to the phenomena in question. Most of the actors have more than one voice, depending on the source (see sources and staging, below.)

The source materials of the play, therefore, are left in their many styles or languages. By languages one can understand methods of communication, public and private, narrative, dramatic, poetic and conversational; their styles and systems, their original and new contexts. The movement of the listener's involvement between the different levels of attention required by each of these forms is the drama of language.

For the director and actors, then, the sources of the lines as in the right margin are not merely historical footnotes but inform the levels of reality of the role being played, so that there are clues to the audience about information such as whether a line came out of someone's mouth or is being put there, ironically or authoritatively.

The source sculptures, too, are a form of stage directions or dramaturgical information.

In counterbalance to this, therefore, I originally provided a minimum of stage directions, as the text's internal order indicates the atemporal and aspatial dynamic of both imagined and actual voices and interpretations of the subject and themes. The dramatic situations could be overlaid on the text or derived from it, as the next, dramaturgical or staging interpretation, both at variance and in harmony with the apparent realities indicated by the text. However, I subsequently added suggested staging directions within the scenes, since it was felt in workshops that these would facilitate keeping track of the characters' parallel realities in a primary reading; but they are not necessarily determinate, particularly in the Parodos.

The name-letter in the left margin is the actor who is speaking. If more than one actor will be speaking the same text, both or all are given.

Each role has a particular configuration of voices. See the character list above, general points given under roles and voices below and details in the notes for each scene.

When the speaking subject changes with the change of voice, this is not necessarily conversational, and the subjects may be, for example, either in different realities, joined by textual tangents or parallels, or following their own trains of thought while in the same situation. When there is more than one speaker of the same speech, there may be two subjectivites in agreement, one influencing the other for example; or there may again be two parallel realities in which the same words have different resonance, one perhaps having originated the text that is put into the mouth of the other. When one speaker is joined by another, the first may continue as if uninterrupted, while the second may begin as if at the beginning of a speech, in his or her own cadences.

The method of simultaneous speech reflects the origins of the writing as mentioned above; for example if P is speaking at the same time as C, then this speech is probably taken from a character in one of Paul Claudel's plays who seems to embody an imagination of his sister by the author; if A speaks in concert with other voices, then the text is probably taken from some expository writing, though inserted into the drama. The director may decide to make one voice subsidiary; or two voices may be speaking the same text in different simultaneous scenes, or in the same scene with different intentions.

The nature of the text is often deliberately anachronistic in order, particularly near the beginning and the end, in keeping with my understanding of the Camille Claudel phenomenon as a victim of interpretation, (like all reconstructive biography) although the scenes of the play have a central chronological development. This, besides making the Parodos reflect the Exodos, which embeds the play in choric interpretation, is to show the fact that much of what is shown is necessarily projected or derived through the filter of time, both backwards and forwards.

Staging, therefore, within the scenes, can often, if

wished, provide a narrative content above and beyond that contained in the text (see Sources above); this may even run contrary to, in the sense of not illustrative of, the actual text at a given moment, as the characters are often speaking of another time and place to the one in which they find themselves. As the staging may be more naturalistic than the text, (or vice versa), so it may also be more chronological, (or less). Visible scenes, too, may be simultaneous.

For the same reasons, actors not speaking should probably be visible according to their influence as much as their realistic presence; the mother speaks little but is a strong force behind C and P, negative or otherwise.

Besides narrative, the staging can also provide the relevant sculptural qualities, including references to or embodiments of the sculptures of C (and R); this also may be a use of uninvolved actors.

ACTORS ACTING ACTORS

There are certain passages in the text where the actors speak at a level outside of the historical sources for the characters, using texts chosen by myself as an author from transcriptions of tapes made by the first cast.

These sections are not to represent a "true" level as opposed to an artificial level, nor particularly for the actors to express what they feel is a more "correct" or more personal opinion reflecting themselves; rather than making a comment on the real actor, they create a fictional, but contemporary actor for the time of the play, between the real and the historical. The passages were chosen for certain reasons: 1) to flow with or complement the thematic dynamism of the text at these points, and 2) for the naturalistic or contemporary speech patterns, including all the doubt, contradiction, and idiosyncracies of the speaker—these used for their particular linguistic textures, reflecting fictionally onto the characters, while different from their more historical/public speech, and often ironically. They would probably work best played at a different register from the other sources—more self-involved or unselfconscious—the distinction in texture enriching further the levels of "reality" operant in the play. I often used forms of speech which revealed to me possible connections between the invented "actor" and the character, which may have been secondary to the real actor's intention in the original context. They don't, on the whole, particularly intend to make the actor/character sound good, and they are not intended to express content in the "best" (most transparent) form.

The passages are also not occasions for improvisation on a theme in performance, which tends to proliferate and give a quite other texture than speech chosen from recorded speech. True improvised speech occurs in the Prologue and Epilogue, where the actors do appear and leave as themselves.

In the Prologue, the true improvisation develops into (and in the Epilogue comes back out from) phrases from such passages, foreshadowing and echoing their appearance inside the text.

ROLES AND VOICES

Characters given in parentheses are either an actor playing a slightly different role, such as A as the father, or appearing only as invented commentary within a scene, such as J as a female counterbalance to A at the end.

The simultaneous speech also provides a choric role. Appropriately to the title of this piece, and unlike the usual role of a chorus, the chorus are predominant and subjective, and their commentary participates in the action.

Some variations on levels of roles/voices for each actor are specified in the notes at the beginning of each scene, or through the source notes.

P, for example, has several linked personalities: as the actor; as author, and therefore as his characters; as art critic; as commentator on staging; and as P the man in relation to the present drama of characters.

On the whole, P's position towards C is that of one trying to liberate himself, as C tries to do from R. One aspect of this is his being her, in which he is not liberated but trying to usurp her perceptions etc. This is reinforced by putting a lot of words into her mouth, but also by identity with her feminine position, to the point of homoeroticism, sublimated into religion; this in the plays, and criticism. In his actual memoirs, though, he is more denying of this, asserting his own hold on reality and devaluing art; so he's away a lot.

The principal subsidiary voice is the Father—he may appear at the beginning, in unison with C as having provided her education, through A and/or P (the use of both voices will avoid over-identification with the individual). Thereafter he is mainly referred to by other characters, either as himself or through literary recurrences— e.g. linked with Atlas in Gorgon myth, or as the father in P's writings. P may also embody him in family matters such as the introduction of R to the family (scene 2). When P has to both speak of his father and speak his words (at the end of scene 4), however, the distinction can be made as if he is reading the father's letter.

170

Besides not trying to be biographically exhaustive, I am not trying to be fair to individuals. It's been tried, and as I also said above, it's suspect and I'd rather say that larger issue in the play. Not only are we responsible for history, but it's not over.

MAIN BIBLIOGRAPHICAL SOURCES
ABBREVIATED IN MARGIN NOTES

JC = Jacques Cassar, *Dossier Camille Claudel*, Livre de Poche

1RMP = Reine-Marie Paris, *Camille Claudel* (family-approved biography), Gallimard

2RMP = Reine-Marie Paris, *l'Oeuvre de Camille Claudel* (catalogue raisonnée)

Paul C = Paul Claudel, *Ma Soeur Camille*; *Camille Claudel Statuaire*; *Journal* all from Pleiade Editions—*Oeuvre*; *Mes Idées sur le Théâtre*, Gallimard
    References to the plays of Paul Claudel—*Tête d'Or*, *L'Annonce Faite à Marie*, *Partage de Midi*, *Violaine* etc are mainly to the Livre de Poche editions.

G = Gsell, *Rodin on Art*, tr. Richard Howard, Horizon

Be = John Berger, *Rodin*, essay

Brigitte Fabre Pellerin, *Le Jour et la Nuit de Camille Claudel* Catalogue of exhibition of Camille Claudel's work Hamburg 1990

K = Sandor Kuthy, *Auguste Rodin und Camille Claudel*, in German

CB = Christine Battersby, *Gender & Genius*

All translations from French, German and Latin are the present author's, unless noted.

GREEN INTEGER
Pataphysics and Pedantry

Douglas Messerli, *Publisher*

Essays, Manifestos, Statements, Speeches, Maxims,
Epistles, Diaristic Notes, Narratives, Natural Histories,
Poems, Plays, Performances, Ramblings, Revelations
and all such ephemera as may appear necessary
to bring society into a slight tremolo of confusion
and fright at least.

*

Green Integer Books